CANOEING AROUND THE CAI~~

A circumnavigati~

———

Robbie ~

First published in 2015 with the help of:
Lumphanan Press
Roddenbrae, Lumphanan,
Aberdeenshire, AB31 4RN

www.lumphananpress.co.uk

© Robbie Nicol 2015

Second Edition printed 2016

My thanks to Eric Bogle for his permission to use the deeply moving lyrics in his song *No Man's Land/The Green Fields of France*.

Thanks also to Brian McNeil for permission to use the gritty social and historical commentary found in his song *No Gods and Precious Few Heroes*, and to Grian Music who publish it.

I would also like to acknowledge Davy Steele's version of the traditional sea shanty *Heave Ya Ho*, as sung on the Battlefield Band's album *Rain, Hail or Shine*.

Printed and bound by:
Imprint Digital, Upton Pyne, Devon, UK.

ISBN: 978-0-9927468-6-5

To family and friends – yours aye.

Contents

Foreword 7

Acknowledgements 11

Introduction 13

1. Going against the flow 19
2. Nature for sale 29
3. The canoeist and the economist 47
4. Time and cycles 67
5. Me and my shadow 80
6. Paradigms lost and found 97
7. The changing climate 115
8. Learning outside the box 128
9. Mind, matter and motorbikes 148
10. The hidden connection 168
11. The connected self 188
12. An adventure too far? 209
13. The end is nigh 226

Epilogue 241

References 245

Map 1 – Circumnavigation 17

Map 2 – Inverness to the Atlantic 18

Map 3 – The Atlantic to the North Sea 114

Map 4 – The coastal passage 200

Foreword

For many canoeists their journeys begin with an idea, and then the research starts with maps and, where possible, guidebooks. Whilst Robbie Nicol informed his 700km journey through maps and texts, it is first and foremost a 'book of the heart' resonant with Robbie's love of his homeland and of his workplace – the Cairngorm Mountains of Scotland. It is also a 'book of the head', a deep thought-piece, an 'inner-journey', a pilgrimage to explore his own, and our relationships with 'nature'.

Nonetheless the journey itself is a remarkable one, crossing Scotland twice by canoe is no small feat as the boat and the paddler's equipment and food must be pushed, dragged or carried uphill before the flow of the rivers can be employed to take it down again towards the sea. And the sea journeys are none the less demanding – solo sea paddling is a very serious undertaking, and Robbie's tale makes plain that that a safe and successful outcome cannot be guaranteed.

During a journey of this type the careful observer will come to know a landscape intimately. And whilst the journey was always intended to provide Robbie with this opportunity, it is as much a journey 'into the self' as it is a journey into, through and even perhaps 'with' a landscape and seascape. It is a characteristic of Robbie's personality that he 'lives deliberately', and his exploration of self is a remarkably thoughtful discussion of what it means to be aware of, come to terms with and indeed act in the context of the current global 'sustainability' crisis. His efforts to understand and find positive ways of both thinking about such issues and then to turn them into a working approach to education resonate with his personal qualities of sensitivity, sincerity and rigour.

Many people have made parts of this physical journey, but as far as I am aware none has linked them together – not that it really matters to Robbie as he has no concern with being 'the first'; but the linking together of the range of fields and concepts of the intellectual journey in this book probably is 'a first'. He draws together and links philosophy, economics, ecology, geology, Earth systems, climate science, sustainable development, literature, cultural history, and music to develop a picture of the Cairngorms area within its global context – rather like looking at a beautiful satellite image or map with all of its complexity evident in the detail that make the whole greater than the sum of the parts. However, this is not an analysis as much as a tale of a physical and intellectual adventure – in the true sense of the word – where the outcome is always uncertain, for both Robbie and his story.

The scale of the undertaking and the demands of the journey resonate with sheer 'graft' – Robbie makes himself work intellectually as much as he works physically – testing his thoughts, formulated over years of careful study and reflection, through the rigours of the journey, and against what he has learned from his 'teachers' and the literature; completing the cycle like the excellent researcher he is by asking his peers for comment… even at the end of this intellectual and physical journey Robbie is still at heart, a learner.

And yet the attention to detail and sensitivity of the discourse is perhaps the most abiding memory the reader may take from this book, his upset at the abuse of a dead whale on the beach, his need to buy a newspaper to put his own problems on the journey into perspective by reading of other people's concerns, and his bemusement at being overtaken by a fly!

Never one to avoid asking himself the awkward questions, he asks if this is just a self-indulgent adventure, concluding that for it to have meaning his learning must be translated into action in his everyday life. Whilst Robbie probably needed to write the book for himself, whether or not there would be other readers, this is manifestly an educational endeavour – and he encourages us in this process through his passion as an outdoor environmental educator, and for his place – Scotland. The central purpose of the book is indeed to be read, and anyone who does so will be inspired with the message that spending time with and as part of 'nature', is essential to learning to care for our planet, our home.

Peter Higgins
Professor of Outdoor and Environmental Education
Director of the United Nations Centre (Scotland)
University of Edinburgh

Acknowledgements

I would like to thank Jimmy Center, who introduced me to canoeing; Mike Redpath, who was a great supporter of our canoe club; Malcolm Foley, the programme leader who took a chance in providing me with a place on an undergraduate degree when I had no school qualifications; Barry Smith, Nev Crowther and Pete Higgins, who you will meet later; all of whom inspired me to experience the beauty and wonder of the outdoors.

There are also individuals and organisations to thank for assisting me with the logistics of *Canoeing around the Cairngorms*. George Reid, Jas Hepburn and Anna Gordon were a mine of information and provided me with books about the landscape I'd be passing through and helped in route planning. The wonderfully innovative, environmentally conscious, award winning travel company Wilderness Scotland provided me with a VHF radio. The super competent mountain and canoe guide Pete Gwatkin lent me sea kayak safety gadgets and my employer, The University of Edinburgh, provided various items of outdoor equipment.

During the journey there were occasions where I was thankful to my wife, Jane, for meeting me along the way to make sure I was stocked with nutritious food and crucially to ensure my electronic diary notes were safely transferred to a laptop. I would also like to thank the film production company, Triple Echo, who had sufficient belief in the concept behind the journey that they filmed part of it for the BBCs Adventure Show.

When writing the book several people provided me with

assistance. Ern Emmet helped me identify the fungas gnat which came to play a large part in the narrative. Also thanks to Paul Stonehouse, whose knowledge and wisdom led me to Henry David Thoreau's ideas that provided the inspiration for the subtitle of this book and its core message. A second thank you to Jane for her help with maps, diagrams and illustrations, and for finding the publishing house Lumphanan Press, whose location appositely lies in the heart of the Cairngorms.

This is an unconventional book and it was with some degree of anxiety that I looked for people to provide critical but helpful commentary on early drafts. For making time within their own busy schedules I would like to thank Simon Beames, Dennis Buchan, Jim Cheney, Nev Crowther, Pete Higgins, Jane Nicol, Roger Scrutton, Graham Harrison-Smith, Barry Smith and John Taylor.

It might not be conventional for an author to thank people who may appear unrelated to their book but in a world in desperate need of role models and leadership I would like to acknowledge those whose writing and actions have inspired me. I would like to pay my respects to the life and achievements of Mahatma Gandhi who believed in peaceful protest to get his way, and to Nelson Mandela who had to bend the rules to get his. The civil rights leader Maya Angelou and political activist Aung San Suu Kyi remain enduring and redoubtable figures in the face of oppression and inequality. Also to the Norwegian writer and mountaineer Arne Naess who worked tirelessly to make the world a better place. Finally, and closer to home, Scotland has had its own share of leaders. W. H. (Bill) Murray has been an inspiration for environmental campaigners and John Smyth continues to be remembered as one of the founding fathers of environmental education.

Introduction

I SET OUT ON A SEVEN-HUNDRED-KILOMETRE, THIRTY-DAY solo journey by canoe and sea kayak around the highest upland mountain plateau in the British Isles – Scotland's Cairngorm Mountains, famous for including some of the tallest peaks in the UK and some of the oldest rock surfaces in Europe. Together with glacial landforms and sub-arctic ecology they provide a unique landmass.

At first this seems a strange prospect since there is no obvious water route to follow. But there is a route. The journey involved canoeing in storm-tossed seas and fierce white water, adventures that were punctuated by the necessity of having to carry my equipment and craft over long stretches of land to link up waterways. I followed a route which, as far as I know, has never been completed in its entirety before.

The fact that I began on April Fools' day was not lost on me. I had intended training over the whole winter to be in good physical shape for this trip. I had also wanted to test myself in large surf and breaking waves, sure in the knowledge that at some stage I'd experience such conditions, either during a passage or landing on a storm beach in an emergency. However, work commitments prevented me from doing any training at all, resulting in my complete lack of physical and mental preparation.

On the plus side I had been a canoeist for twenty years and had experience of kayaking grade five white water and paddling in force eight conditions at sea. While I wouldn't by choice be in these conditions on this journey I knew that I'd only be one bad decision away from something serious happening to me. I comforted myself with the knowledge that I had been leading kayaking and canoeing groups fairly regularly in the time running up to my departure, even though the conditions were not nearly as severe as I could expect on this trip. I reasoned that if the conditions were difficult at sea I wouldn't go out and if the river rapids were too difficult I'd walk round them.

I also took comfort in the knowledge that all decisions were mine to take and that I would be in control of my own destiny. However, this responsibility brought with it a number of consequences. The first was that if anything went wrong there would be no-one to blame but me, and the second was that whatever might go wrong there was only me to sort things out. In other words I was to be alone.

Canoeing around the Cairngorms describes not just an adventure, but also a journey of discovery to find out more about the magnificent landscape I passed through. The book is an attempt to bring the land alive by exploring its natural and cultural stories – the flora, fauna, geology, biology, its history of war and peace and the people (past and present) of this remarkable area. I make no claims to be an expert in any of these subjects; I am more someone trying to understand the world around me.

Another purpose of the journey was to spend time thinking about what has come to be described as 'the environmental crisis'. I knew that research shows that polar ice sheets are melting. I had read too of the loss of biodiversity around the world, of poverty and famine, depletion of natural resources, pollution and a whole host of depressing subjects. As an observer of how society responds to these issues I worried, and still do, about the lack of political initiative and slow speed at which change comes about. In my work as an outdoor environmental education lecturer and researcher I had become increasingly concerned that education systems around the world are not doing a very good job of encouraging people to live sustainable lifestyles.

Part of the problem is that most people in industrialised and post-industrialised nations do not spend much time outdoors. There is a link between the absence of direct experience with nature and unsustainable lifestyles. Related to this is the way we talk about these things in a detached and highly abstract manner, where nature remains remote from people's everyday lives. I wanted to develop a discourse that recognised the seriousness of the situation we find ourselves in but without the 'doom and gloom' focus.

So the journey's dual purpose meant that on the one hand it was a physical journey, since it could be traced on a map, and readily characterised by the trials and tribulations associated with outdoor adventures. On the other hand it was a metaphorical journey, or an inner journey, which combined to satiate the inner needs of health, happiness and well-being through a purposeful and protracted engagement with nature. It involved a search for meaning within the beauty and inspiration of the land and seascape. It was a quest to look for purpose in a contemporary world characterised by a changing atmosphere, degraded landscapes, reduced biodiversity and yet infinite beauty. Essentially it was a pilgrimage to explore the essence of my own, and by extension humanity's, relationship with nature. The purpose of this book is to communicate these experiences because, as a species, we venture forth into the future towards an unknown destination. Our journey is a shared one.

In planning the book I had to develop a 'voice' with which to 'speak'. However I was also *travelling* 'in the first person', with no-one else to talk to, and I feared that the writing style would become a monologue. I have resolved this difficulty by introducing a cast of characters. At various stages of my life I have met individuals who have profoundly affected what I think about. To acknowledge these contributions I have used their voices as well as my own to create contrast within the text. While these are 'real' people when they 'speak', their contributions are based on my own memories of past conversations. I have endeavoured to be accurate in my recollections and any errors are entirely my own responsibility.

Map 1 – Circumnavigation

Map 2 – Inverness to the Atlantic

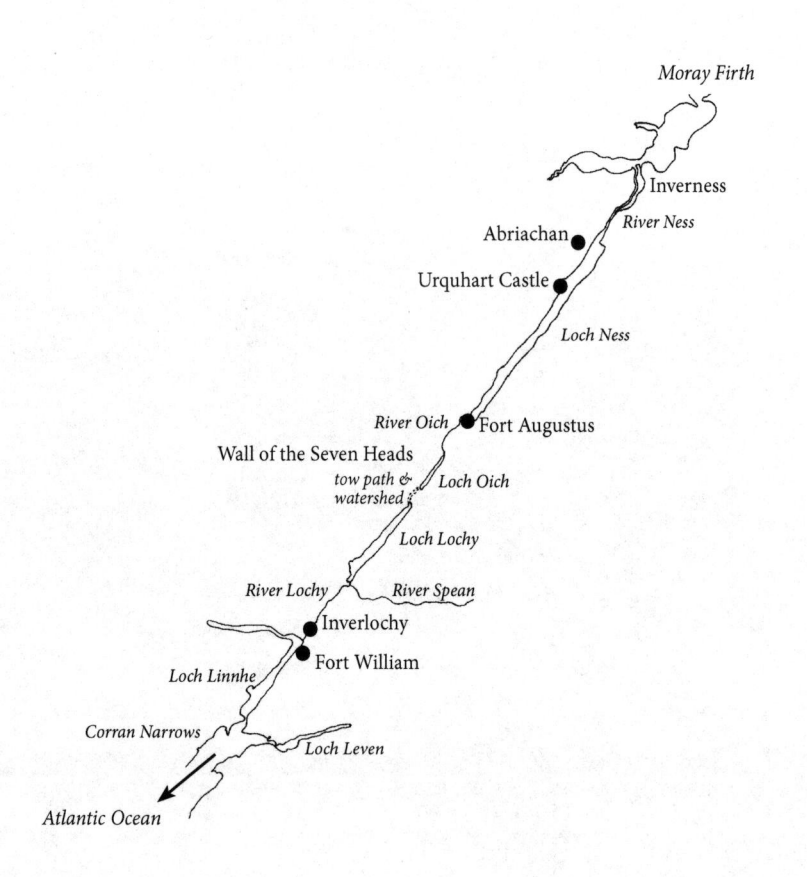

1

Going against the flow

It was 6 a.m. The first photograph in the plate section shows me standing beside my canoe ready to embark. In the background the sea is almost still with only a light breeze gently rippling its flat surface. My right hand is holding a wooden paddle and my left is bunched in a fist, trying to avoid the penetrating grip of the cold. The temperature that day was −4°C. I remember leaving home early in the morning, driving past the Cairngorm Mountains and seeing a red glow over the hills as the sun rose behind them. The redness, the cloudless sky and the dry windless cold were a sure sign of a high-pressure weather system and a bright day ahead.

Despite the penetrating cold it was a beautiful morning as I pushed off from the shore, with the sun just creeping above the horizon. Wispy strands of light haar were everywhere and I eagerly awaited the full arrival of the sun to evaporate the thin veil that prevented its warming rays from reaching me.

In this expectant state I paddled into the mouth of the River

Ness through the harbour at Inverness and began the ascent, by water and portage, of the Great Glen watershed. Inverness is an industrial harbour and so my horizon was filled with cargo freight and the long arms of cranes. I felt a little rebellious as I passed by the green-slimed walls of the piers towering high above me. Harbour masters tend not to like small craft like mine getting in the way of container ships and interfering with the serious work of industry.

There was no sign of the harbour master and my thoughts drifted towards Barry and his influence on my life. My formal education came a little later in life than for most university students. Leaving school at fifteen without any qualifications I spent the next fourteen years working as a soldier, driver, labourer and sports centre attendant. I don't know where the desire to learn really came from but I do know that it came. I stepped into another world when I was accepted to read a degree in recreation management at Moray House College, now part of the University of Edinburgh. During those studies I encountered the world of books and found out about sociology, psychology, philosophy and management. My undergraduate years fanned the flames of an already naturally curious mind.

And it wasn't just about books: there were inspirational lecturers too. Barry was one of those. At first it wasn't clear to me why these lecturers stood out from the rest. However, as my four-year course unfolded the reasons for my preferences became increasingly apparent. The common factor among my favourites was that they all had a passion for working with people in the outdoors. This encouraged me to find out more about 'the outdoors' as a place of learning.

With this heady mix of the outdoors and book learning it wasn't long before I found myself on a solo walking trip among the plateaux and valleys of various mountains with E. F. Schumacher's *Small is Beautiful* in my rucksack. On one level the walk was an adventure involving airy ridge scrambles and navigation in difficult mountain terrain. At another level it was, as Robert Pirsig described metaphorically in *Zen and the Art of Motorcycle Maintenance*, a journey into the 'high country of the mind'.

Both of these were seminal texts for me and I began to recognise that abstract learning did not have to take place indoors. In hindsight, this was an important step in building the motivations for my navigation around the Cairngorms. So it was with curiosity in abundance that I started out on my journey, armed with ideas and the time to think about them.

Up-river of the harbour I confronted the first of many obstacles presented to me by the river: a tidal rapid. When the tide is fully in the water level covers the rocky rapid, but when the tide is fully out the water is left to flow over a steep river-wide drop created by large angular boulders. These are part of the foundations of the bridge and are not a natural part of the riverbed. I decided to portage the rapid via the base of one of the bridge arches. I doubt the architects, engineers and labourers ever imagined that the bridge they built for crossing the river could actually act as a bridge for upstream travel as well. Portaging is a wonderful example of the versatility of my craft – I can move my own seventy-six kilogramme bulk, forty kilogrammes of equipment and another thirty-two kilogrammes of canoe upstream over an otherwise un-navigable river rapid.

Above the rapid the current flowed strongly and although I could make some progress upstream with the use of my paddle, I needed to find a more efficient method of propulsion.

By attaching a line at the front and back of the canoe it was possible to walk along the bank towing the canoe upstream. For this to work well, I needed to make sure that most of the onboard weight was in the downstream end of the canoe. This allowed the upstream end to sit high in the water and the current to flow underneath. It was then just a matter of using the two lines to set the canoe at an angle so that the current caught and forced the craft out into deeper water where it wouldn't snag on shallow rocks. There is a large degree of subtlety in lining; when you get it right it is almost like taking an obedient dog for a walk on a lead (see photo 2, plate section).

The lower stretch of the River Ness is a wonderful place to line. Miles of grassy banks make progress easy. I moved upstream with a combined mass of one hundred and forty-eight kilogrammes at about three or four miles an hour. Since the average speed of traffic in inner city London is around twelve miles per hour I could feel pretty good about such progress in relation to any internal combustion competitor. Lining really is exquisite, although I'm not sure that the people of Inverness out in the early morning in search of their Sunday newspapers knew what to make of me.

The thought of taking the canoe for a walk draws me inward and for a moment I hear Barry saying, 'You are going the wrong way.' I think I know what he means – people are used to seeing canoes going downstream and not upstream. So to many people going upstream *is* the 'wrong way'. But this observation is only the tip of a very large iceberg. Barry set out to deliberately provoke thinking about thinking. In this case, 'canoeing the wrong way', is simply a metaphor and an invitation to explore life.

It is the versatility of the canoe that made it so useful to hunters and trappers throughout history. In the seventeenth to nineteenth centuries people would make their way into the North American interior, loading up canoes with provisions to sustain them on the way in and furs for sale on the way out. In this way the canoe was a workhorse designed for both upstream and downstream use. Waterways became corridors of access connecting villages further and further inland to vast interiors. The canoe provided the means by which settlement could take place and in time populations became dependent on it for trade in goods and services.

The way a canoe is used nowadays is very different. The River Ness is around ten kilometres long and to canoe its length *with* the flow would take about two hours. The gentle declination of the riverbed allows the water to accelerate on its path towards the sea and provides a ready-made conveyor belt to speed up the canoeist's downstream passage. Thus landscape, gravity and perception combine to provide the modern canoeist with the fundamental truth that the 'right way' to canoe a river is downstream.

It is convenient and common for two or more canoeists to drive to a stretch of river and leave one car at the beginning and another at the end. This degree of organisation allows the maximum time on the water for learning skills, playing in rapids and dropping over waterfalls. Exciting and adventurous as this is, its continued practice reinforces the mindset that the correct way to canoe a river is downstream. Furthermore the river becomes valued directly proportional to the amount of white water on it and so one stretch becomes 'better' than another based on its white-water qualities and its appeal to the adventurer.

In this way the river becomes reduced to units of recreational convenience. One consequence of this is that only bits of the river become known. Thus knowing the river becomes very piecemeal. What is absent from these experiences is seeing the river as a whole (and not just its white-water interests) and seeing it from an upstream perspective as well as a downstream perspective.

This begins to address Barry's observation about going the wrong way, but only in a superficial sense. Barry is less interested in the technical activity and more interested in the 'high country of the mind'. What he is really interested in is how the idea of canoeing upstream relates to people's everyday lives.

It seems to me that there is a parallel between canoeing as practiced today and the way people lead their lives. Canoeing as a 'one way' activity is relatively modern. What the history of canoeing shows us is that people's values shift over time, and this makes me wonder both how society's values change, and whether people actually notice those changes.

In *The Other Side of Eden* Hugh Brody explores, in evolutionary terms, the relationship between humans and the landscape. He suggests that human history can be divided into three notable epochs: hunter-gatherer, agriculturalist and industrialist. By some estimates, the spread of hunter-gathering communities into habitable regions of the world began as much as four hundred thousand years ago. However, the sedentism necessary for agriculture to succeed was clearly apparent ten thousand years ago and by this time agriculture had spread throughout much of the world. The process of change by which countries moved from an agricultural economy to an industrial economy began in Britain around 1750 with the birth of the Industrial Revolution. There are two conclusions to be made from this timeline. The first is as, Hugh Brody points out, that in evolutionary terms we have been hunter-gatherers for far longer than we have been agriculturalists. The second is that we have been industrialists for a far shorter time than for any other dominant epoch. Humans have lived their lives based on a hunter-gatherer and agriculturalist economy for some four hundred thousand years, but as an industrial economy for only just over two hundred and fifty years.

Barry would not be entirely happy with the way this logic is progressing. He would point out that the timeline does not recognise that many countries today exhibit at least two and sometimes three of these epochs simultaneously. Of course, this is true, but before 1750 there was no major industry to affect hunter-gatherers and agriculturalist economies. This is important because the point at which the economy came to be dominated by industry is pivotal in the changing relationship between human beings and the landscape. Even the differences between the hunter-gatherer and agriculturalist epochs were immense. For example, hunter-gatherers' knowledge of the world was based on specific geographies, whereas agriculturalists controlled the landscape through knowledge based on reason and abstraction.

As Brody observes:

> hunter-gatherer knowledge is dependent on the most intimate possible connection with the world and with the creatures that live in it… they also care for it, showing respect and attention to its well-being. All hunter-gatherers had rules about the treatment of the animals they hunted and the plants they gathered – rules that were designed to show and perpetuate goodwill.

Brody makes the point that whereas hunter-gatherers sought to know the land, agriculturalists sought to change it through deforestation, settlement and farming. These changes continued into the industrial epoch as the rhythms of nature were replaced by the factory clock and notions of seasonal time gave way to mechanical time.

The clock and the time it represents, which were supposed to assist order and productivity, became a value in itself. The clock changed the way we think. Instead of crops being planted in accordance with seasonal cycles, populations began to think in terms of being early, on time, or late for work, and leisure time created a dualism between work and non-work. The scientific worldview reinforced this conception of time.

In the seventeenth century René Descartes sought to provide a new way of thinking about the world. His central metaphor was the clock made up of hundreds of different pieces. He compared the Earth to the clock and its pieces to species. The problem with what has become known as 'Cartesian reductionism', as Fritjof Capra has said, is that 'scientists, encouraged by their success in treating living organisms as machines, tend to believe they are *nothing but* machines'. This way of thinking provided the means by which nature could be dominated and controlled. The disconnection between people and land was well underway.

Not long after portaging the bridge I passed by Inverness Castle, which has a prominent statue of Flora MacDonald in its grounds. In 1746 Flora assisted the Jacobite leader Charles Edward Stuart (Bonnie Prince Charlie) after his defeat at the battle of Culloden. The romantic and popular version of events is encapsulated in *The Skye Boat Song*, where the gallant would-be king is spirited away from certain death 'over the sea to Skye' while his loyal followers fought a rear-guard action at Culloden to ensure his escape. Other accounts are less kind. In Brian McNeill's folk song *No Gods and Precious Few Heroes* he suggests the Prince 'ran like a rabbit doon the glen leaving better folk than him to be butchered'. McNeill's lyrics are a gritty reminder of the dangers of glamourising historical accounts when the truth is often far from self-evident.

The river is full of stories. I once stood on the banks as a ten-year-old, fishing rod in hand, filled with excitement at seeing the first salmon that rose to my fly. It was on the River Ness that the first recorded sighting of the Loch Ness monster took place when in AD 563 the missionary St Columba came from Ireland on a currach. Columba landed on the Island of Iona on Scotland's west coast and began to build a monastery as part of his plan to spread the teachings of Christianity. Columba travelled on a coracle to Inverness Castle to meet King Brude, king of the local people who were known as the Picts. On his way down the river he saw the Loch Ness monster attacking a swimmer and used his miraculous powers to chase the monster away. The written account paved the way for the enduring tale of 'Nessie's' existence.

It took a full day to ascend the ten kilometres of the River Ness. I remember that where it opens out into Loch Ness (see photo 3, plate section) I was surrounded by a sense of peace, the endorphins from a full day of making progress upstream filling me with well-being. An unseen woodpecker hammered away at a rotting tree, the echo moving around the forest so that it seemed to come from everywhere at once. Two greater spotted woodpecker (*Dendrocopos major*) males flew past, jostling each other for territory. A grey wagtail (*Motacilla cinerea*) bobbed from stone to stone, weaving a spell of silence, drawing me in.

What I love about travelling in a canoe is the way that you can't force things. You have to be efficient, which means that you need to work with the weight that's in the craft, the current of the river and the force of the wind. If you try to force the canoe to do certain movements in certain conditions you very quickly find that you are just not strong enough. As one coach explained to me, 'It's like paddling a barge with a matchstick.' You need to work with the weight, water and wind. You adapt your strokes, learn to edge the canoe a fraction and move your own weight to change the trim. All the time you are looking for that 'sweet spot' where your forward momentum meets with least resistance. Because the wind and current are always changing, sometimes greatly but often very subtly, your whole being becomes a constant search for that 'sweet spot'. When you realise this you begin carefully, mindfully and beautifully, to work with the forces of nature and not against them. In this way nature is not a combatant or something to be conquered but something to understand, to learn from and to live with.

In his ground-breaking book *Path of the Paddle* Bill Mason says, 'An appreciation of the canoe and acquisition of the necessary skills to utilise it as a way to journey back to what's left of the natural world is a great way to begin this voyage of discovery.' On the first day of my own voyage of discovery I had utilised many of those skills, such as lining, poling, wading and paddling. I set up my tent on the shore of Loch Ness that evening and wondered what else the journey held in store.

2

Nature for sale

Due to its size Loch Ness is more like the open sea than an inland loch to the canoeist. It is thirty-seven kilometres long and two hundred and thirty metres deep, making it the largest by volume stretch of freshwater in the United Kingdom. Looking at it on an Ordnance Survey 1:50,000 map reveals some of its detail. The closeness of the land-based contours are matched by those beneath the water surface, and as you canoe along it is incredible to think that if the water magically disappeared you would freefall two hundred and thirty metres into a sediment layer eight metres deep. If that did not arrest your fall the hard layer of clay below would. If one of the world's tallest buildings, six hundred metres in height, rested its foundations on that clay, half of it would be submerged and half would sit above the water level. And if the glacier that passed by more than ten thousand years ago were still there, none of the building would be visible above the kilometre-thick ice.

The prevailing winds are south-westerly and the loch lies

within a geological fault-line running in the same direction. When the wind blows it gathers the waves before it and the longer the waves travel on the water the bigger they grow. The length of water over which wind travels before it reaches a boat is known to sailors as a 'fetch'. Thirty-seven kilometres is a long fetch so when the wind blows, as it normally does, the loch becomes a restless mass of water, its surface shaped by the ceaseless actions of the wind.

This is not a place to underestimate. On my trip up the River Ness I met a man walking his dog along the banks, a prawn fisherman who seemed rather surprised to see a canoe going upstream. When I explained my intention to canoe the length of Loch Ness he told me that he regularly used the loch as part of his route through the Caledonian Canal system, taking his fishing trawler from his home on the east coast to the fishing grounds off the west coast. One day on entering the loch he was exposed to a seething maelstrom of huge broken waves. A force ten wind had been blowing from the south-west and was being funnelled down the constricted space between the mountains, tossing his trawler around. He told me that with the mountains stretching high on each side and the sky heavily overcast with rain clouds it was like travelling through a dark tunnel. They were the worst conditions he'd ever experienced – and this was someone who had been at sea all his working life.

So I was thankful for the peaceful conditions that I encountered when I set off up the loch, with the lack of wind leaving it flat and calm. The mountains reflected perfectly in the water, stretching equally skywards and down into the depths, the colours absolutely stunning. The tranquillity I felt from my first day up the river continued.

The act of propelling a canoe is not merely functional. One of my paddles is called an otter-tail (see photo 4, plate section). Its long thin shape gives it its name and it is made from a single piece of red cherry. While an otter-tail is ideal for relaxed touring, Bill Mason suggests it is also good for solo ballet. I think I know what he means by solo ballet. A white-water paddle is shorter to avoid hitting rocks on the riverbed and shaped more like a square-edged shovel. However, the otter-tail is long and sinuous and elegant to look at. Pulling it through the water provides forward momentum but it is the retrieval that adds to the beautiful feel. You can retrieve it horizontally, above or in the water, or vertically, and all the strokes have names.

In reality, though, when you use this paddle the strokes become one part of a complex whole as the changing variables of wind, wave and current require you to constantly adapt your stroke. These adaptations are so subtle that someone who has never paddled a canoe would not see the difference. When it is done well the result feels effortless and cathartic. Also, because of these changing variables, the stroke that you set out to do is not necessarily the one you finish with. This subtlety requires constant attention and adaptation to external conditions. When it all comes together paddling the canoe becomes absorbing and compelling.

I remember Barry talking about moments like these. They help to cleanse the mind of everyday clutter and provide quality thinking time. So it was that I drifted back to my thoughts on the three epochs, the relationship between people and nature, and how this relationship can change and yet go unnoticed by society over time. At first it is not really clear how these three issues relate, but I know Barry believed it to involve economics.

Economics can be described as the study of production,

distribution and consumption of goods and services. This description can be used as a lens through which the subsistence activities of the hunter-gatherer, agriculturalist and industrialist can be viewed. The subsistence methods of early hunter-gatherers depended on finding shelter from the elements while going about their everyday life of securing adequate supplies of fresh water for drinking, foraging for edible plants, fishing and hunting for wild animals. Whenever food and water supplies became scarce these communities were free to move to places of abundance. The skills required for this lifestyle included knowing where to look for food and working with raw materials to fashion clothes, tools and weapons. Thus the production, distribution and consumption of goods and services were restricted to what people could carry with them; possessions were minimal. While the population of communities around the world remained small, the effect on the landscape and biodiversity remained in the main minimal and biologically sustainable.

In terms of the relationship between humans and nature, human behaviour was determined largely by environmental conditions such as the availability of food and water. The production, distribution and consumption of goods and services, such as they were, would have been conceptualised as those necessary for immediate bodily needs. Thus the dependence on nature for human needs was direct and apparent as the ability to survive depended on adapting to seasonal variations. Furthermore, the idea of accumulating wealth would have been an alien concept.

The key change that allowed hunter-gatherers to become farmers was the domestication of animals, plants and grains more than ten thousand years ago. The ability to create food surplus through farming and herding created the opportunity for humans to live in larger settlements. As food sources became more abundant and dependable and farming methods more efficient, there was the opportunity for some people to be freed from food production. The development of textiles (e.g. wool, silk, linen and cotton) and trades and crafts (e.g. builders, carpenters, weavers, tailors) and professions (e.g. civil servants, doctors, lawyers) provided a range of goods and services that could be traded. This major re-ordering of society must have had an important consequence for the way in which people viewed nature. While hunter-gatherers had to adapt to environmental conditions, agriculturalists were able to insulate themselves from seasonal differences in temperature, the origins of their food, and ultimately their dependence on nature. This explains Brody's point that whereas hunter-gatherers sought to know the land agriculturalists sought to change it.

Here then are some of the first signs in human history of a break from direct and observable dependence on nature. The produce of nature could now be packaged and sold as the production, distribution and consumption of goods and services increased in scale and scope. The introduction of agriculture dramatically increased levels of economic activity, and in this way nature became a human possession to be bought and fought over. The reciprocity between the hunter-gatherer and nature gave way to a relationship based on possession: through feudal rights and title deeds people began to own nature. Ultimately the possession became inferior to the possessor.

This detached relationship continued into the industrial age and at the same time provided communities around the world with goods and services unimaginable to our hunter-gatherer forefathers. The Industrial Revolution began in Britain in the eighteenth century and spread to many other parts of the globe. The development of agriculture required large numbers of settled populations, and the Industrial Revolution intensified this trend. More importantly it required those populations to be condensed and urban-based, to provide labour for factories and mills. Technological advances, fuelled by the development of the steam engine, increased the rate of industrial-scale manufacturing. Developments in transportation provided the means for the distribution of goods not just to domestic markets, but overseas as well. While these developments brought benefits such as higher living standards and life expectancy (for some people), they caused even greater separation between people and nature, because of the displacement of people from rural to urban living.

As I sat on the bank, coffee in hand, the loch remained flat calm and I watched a power boat passing parallel to the bank. The water looked oily black and the wake from the boat was quite distinct. If I believed in the Loch Ness monster I could easily see the shape of it in the wake – the rounded humps higher than the lower looked so like the elongated humps that Nessie is supposed to have. The movement of the waves as they rolled towards me gave the impression of movement from right to left following the boat that created the wake. I know this is not a romantic view and probably spoils the hope of many believers, nor is it likely to get tourists excited, but I think it is a reasonable explanation for some Nessie sightings.

Another explanation is that circus owners are known to have stopped their trucks on hot days to let their elephants cool down by swimming in the loch. It is quite feasible that passing motorists who only had a momentary glimpse through the trees could have confused the elephants' shapes for that of a monster. Who after all would expect to see elephants swimming in a Scottish loch? Divers have also reported seeing very large eels in the loch and this may explain at least some of the underwater sightings. Decomposition on the loch bed causes large gaseous disturbances as the bubbles break the surface with almighty flatulent releases. Seals have also been known to make their way up the River Ness and into Loch Ness following the Atlantic salmon and they, like otters when they break the surface to swim, could easily account for some of the sightings.

I don't want to leave this account of Nessie sightings with an overly rational explanation that leaves no room for the possibility of its existence because, even though I have not seen it, I believe I may have had a close encounter. In June 1993 my wife Jane and I had been canoeing down Loch Ness's south shore and we decided to cross the loch to visit Urquhart Castle. It is an ancient building, the present castle dating back to at least the thirteenth century. Before that it was the site of a Pictish fort at the time Columba passed by on his way to meet King Brude. The old red sandstone ruins of Urquhart Castle remain very impressive and are owned by the National Trust for Scotland. Being next to a busy road it is a very popular stop for coach tours. It is also a favourite Nessie sighting spot. As we paddled across the loch we could see the battlements full of people peering through their binoculars and the buzz of excitement was loud enough to reach us across the water. Clearly the audience were disappointed as the twin-humped monster separated itself into single independent humps when we stepped out of the canoe onto the shore.

But the story does not end there. We continued our journey to Inverness and next day bought a newspaper. One of the headlines was 'Nessie sightings claim by couple'. One witness said that there was a massive bow wave coming off the front of the monster and another said that it left a huge wake that crashed onto the beach as it passed. Since the time coincided precisely with our positions on the loch it would appear that either the witnesses mistook us for Nessie or, since we did not see Nessie ourselves, it must have been behind us. I like to think that it was chasing us without us knowing and despite the speed that it must have been doing to create a 'massive bow wave' and 'huge wake' it still could not keep up.

There is a difference between paddling out in the middle of the loch and paddling close to the side. In the middle you get little sense of moving, but close to the bank you get a distinct sense of progress because the proximity to the bank means that you see trees, rocks and headlands slipping by. The different sensation had an effect on me and when I was close to the bank I wanted to go faster as I experienced the sense of making way. To preserve my peaceful aesthetic I stayed away from the sides and progressed down the middle of the loch which, thanks to the multi-dimensional reflections and merging of the water and sky, gave the appearance of a road.

Many writers assert that we have now moved beyond the industrialist epoch into a post-industrial era, changing from a manufacturing based economy to a service-based economy. While this is undoubtedly true, I stick to the term 'industrial economy' because there is little evidence that post-industrial society has significantly altered the relationship between humanity and nature.

McNeill, in his *Something New under the Sun*, says that:

for many millions of years the Earth's land, air, water and living things have functioned in a complex evolving harmony, punctuated by occasional collisions with asteroids. Human action has added a new voice to that harmony, originally a soft one easily compatible with the others.

These words imply that this voice is now no longer soft, making us question what humanity's contemporary relationship with nature is, as well as what needs to change in order for us to live harmoniously.

Economists have suggested that for some time now humans have been living on the capital of nature. Looking at the hunter-gatherer, agriculturalist and industrialist epochs it is fair to say that in order to subsist the communities in all three depended on nature's capital, such as food and raw materials. However, there are other factors to consider here. The first is one of scale. The scale of use of nature as capital has increased throughout the three epochs. The second is that as economic systems developed around the world, particularly in the industrial epoch, they failed to factor in the two key concepts of depletion and pollution. The definition of economic activity as the production, distribution and consumption of goods and services does not fully account for all of the consequences of activity in an industrial economy. More specifically the true ecological costs of economics are not factored into the equation.

As we have seen, economies throughout the epochs are based on the planet's productivity. However, the economies of industrial nations are no longer based around subsistence needs but around the concept of economic growth. Economies are often assessed by looking at the Gross Domestic Product (GDP) which measures the value of all goods and services produced by the economic activity within a country. In this way a monetary value can be placed on a country's economic success, but there is one more factor to consider, by far the most important. Within this model of valuation a country's existing wealth is never enough. It is an inherent value of the system that a successful economy depends on *growth*. People are encouraged to buy more so that the economy grows.

As the Canadian scientist and environmental activist David Suzuki points out in *Time to Change*, this method of measurement 'is devoid of assessment of the social and environmental costs associated with the increase in goods and services'. In support of his theory he asks his readers to consider the case of the 1989 *Exxon Valdez* oil spill in Alaska, which he describes as the greatest marine disaster in American history. One thousand miles of pristine coastline were affected, and more than two hundred and fifty thousand birds, one thousand rare sea otters and an unknown number of other animals were killed. Thousands of workers were required for the clean-up operation, which contributed to America's GDP. In this way natural disasters are 'good' for the economy because they create employment and result in an increase in the trade of goods and services. Thus Suzuki concludes that such measurements do 'not even register the quality and quantity of clean air, water, soil, and biological diversity'.

The use of economic growth as a measure of progress is akin to false accounting. This is because many of the Earth's resources are finite even though economic theory does not operate on that principle. For example, it takes millions of years for plant material to form fossil fuels. Once it has been extracted and used it would take a similar time to form again. Therefore the application of economics is based on the false assumption that nature is endlessly renewable. However, as Suzuki states:

> we have an absolute requirement for air, water, soil, and biodiversity and other living things for our health and survival. Thus the biophysical elements of the planet are fundamental capital that make our society and lives possible and should be the foundation for all our spiritual and material value, including economics.

The problem with growth economics, therefore, is that it allows us to treat nature as though it were a commodity. When we treat nature as goods to be produced, distributed and consumed it becomes possible to psychologically distance ourselves from nature, thus creating the impression that it belongs to us to use in ways that are profitable. Thus industrial economies have grown out of all proportion to the subsistence activities of hunter-gatherers. In other words growth economics serves to increase the perception of separation from nature when in fact human beings have a biological dependence on nature.

I wonder what Barry would make of my analysis: I guess he would consider it a little superficial. I could also imagine him saying, 'You criticise the existing system but offer no alternatives. The world is full of people who are good at identifying problems, but where are the solutions in your analysis? What about the argument that changing economic systems is beyond the power of individuals?'

However, it is important to point out that a problem exists. A problem that is not recognised as a problem is an even bigger problem. It is important also to stand up and be counted, to voice your concerns even if you don't have all the answers. It is not easy sticking your head above the parapet to speak out, particularly when your ideas may be a challenge to people's lifestyles.

With a very light tail wind picking up I raised my sail. The wind was not strong enough to be the sole method of propulsion though, so I paddled too. Sail-assisted and paddling my heart out I was overtaken by a fly. The indignation of being overtaken by such a paltry specimen tempted me to paddle faster but my ego subsided as I proved no match for my competitor who cheekily landed on the sail and hitched a ride for the rest of the morning. Its presence was fascinating. There were lots of them around, as though part of a hatch. My friend was 5–6 mm in length (excluding wings). Most fascinating of all was I had no idea what this fly was called.

This caused me to think of another of my lecturers. Nev is a field biologist who inspired students on field trips with his mesmerising knowledge of flora and fauna. There is a view in environmental education that the naming of species is not important and that it is more important for the learner to experience the essences of species without the need to learn complicated names, particularly scientific names. I am not convinced by this argument. My disagreement is not whether names should be taught so much as I think the argument misses a much bigger point. Whether to name or not arises out of a confusion between teaching and learning. The more important question is: 'Will the learner learn more about a species, and its relationship with other species, if a name is used or if it is not?' Looking at the debate this way implies that the teacher has to find out more about how their learners learn than imposing a generalised belief in any particular method of teaching that assumes learners' learn in the same way and at the same speed.

This way of learning is different from the method of establishing logical principles based on what you know already. What I wanted to learn about this fly could not rely on the logical process of arriving at conclusions from premises. You can't just think this fly's name, or its ecological niche, into existence. A body of knowledge will exist about this fly even though I do not have the details at my fingertips. There are some things we can learn from thinking alone and some things we need external input from books or teachers.

This led me to think of another of my inspiring lecturers. I can imagine steam coming out of Pete's ears on this particular issue. Pete has always argued that scientific names create a universal language that is understood regardless of national language. For example in the English language there is a bird called a 'swift'. The same bird in the Swedish language is called 'tornsvala' but its scientific name of *Apus apus* is used in both Swedish, English and indeed all languages. Pete also told me about a breed of fish in these waters known as a 'pike'. Its scientific name is *Esox lucius*, with lucius being a reference to Lucifer the devil. Rows of needle sharp teeth and a highly predatory nature provide hints as to why it has been called colloquially the 'wolf' or 'devil fish'. While these names are overly sensationalist and misleading in an ecological sense they may just provide the non-scientist with the curiosity to find out more.

Anyway, back to the fly. To my untrained eye it looked like a fly but scientifically I don't really know what a fly is. I knew that a fly was considered a winged insect but then I wasn't even sure scientifically what a winged insect was. I guess it was the myriad of species that enthused the Swedish scientist Carl Linnaeus to set about developing a system for naming, ranking and classifying organisms. The problem, for me, was that I did not have any of the modern field guides based on Linnaeus' taxonomy to help me identify the fly. So I took a photograph to help me identify it when I got home (see photo 5, plate section).

Later when I showed the photograph to a few experts the response was astonishing. There are several thousands of species similar to this, not all of which have been identified. The best guess was that it was a species known as a fungus gnat belonging to the family *mycetophilidae*. When I enquired further I found that there are likely just a few United Kingdom experts on this group and they would not be able to identify it from a photo. They would need to dissect it and check its genitalia. Despite three hundred years of taxonomic study this fly cannot be identified by observation alone.

Trying to find out the name of something has been important. Even though I still don't know its name the process of trying to find out has led me to learn so much more about it. It seems that what is important is not whether I am able to identify and name something, so much as to work out what inspires me to learn more. I imagine my absent mentors nodding. It is not easy keeping diverse strands of thought going at once. What for example has industrial economics got to do with fungus gnats and different ways of learning? Barry, Pete and Nev used to like setting these sorts of puzzles.

With so much to think about and in anticipation of writing this book I carried a digital recorder to record my thoughts. It was amazing how often I had to take it out of my buoyancy aid pocket, remove it from its waterproof case, switch it on and speak into it. The frequency with which I had to perform this ritual was an indication of the stimulation my journey invoked. My internal landscape was alive with conversations and spontaneous intrusions such as the meeting with the fungus gnat. The outer water and landscapes bombarded my senses and the inner landscape was always restless as it attempted to process and make sense of these welcome intrusions.

With so much to make sense of I was reminded of something the Himalayan mountaineer Doug Scott once said at a public lecture. He was asked what he thought about when he was storm bound for days at a time in a tent on the exposed ridge of some mountain. He said, 'It is not so much the thoughts that are important but the pauses between them'. The Norwegian philosopher Arne Naess was of a similar view when he said, 'Even a whole stream of thought might occur to one, but it is the pauses and the internal silence that are the hallmarks of this kind of relationship with nature... as a person, one is completely absorbed.'

Part of making sense of difficult multi-layered concepts is to keep them in abeyance at times, to savour the thinking that speeding up could lead to premature conclusions. There is more potential for this sort of slow thinking when you are alone. Put another way, you are never alone because the absence of something means the presence of something else. In this situation the absence of people enhances the presence of thoughts. Spending time alone is vastly underrated.

I had made good progress and looked for a campsite towards the end of Loch Ness. I wanted to avoid the north side where the main road runs so looked for something a little quieter on the south shore. A rocky ledge was all I could find in the failing light and it was completely unsuitable for erecting a tent. A large tree trunk, washed up from some recent storm, lay across the rocky ledge and I positioned my canoe parallel to it, tying a tarpaulin between the two to provide a shelter (see photo 6, plate section). With lots of driftwood around it was not long before I had a fire going to brew some tea.

Staring into a fire is hypnotic. One cannot help but be absorbed by its presence. It is impossible to sit by a fire and not poke it, fiddle with it and feed it with more wood. I guess this is what Doug Scott meant where the pauses are as important as the thoughts themselves. The presence of a fire instills a way of being that cleanses the mind of difficult thoughts, sometimes offering moments of clarity that can only happen when the clutter is removed. It is almost as though the thoughts themselves get in the way of making sense of them. Perhaps the flames of the fire help burn away the shells of conscious thought and help to reveal the seeds of truth inside.

Think of hunter-gatherers sitting around their fires all those years ago – was their quality of life so much inferior to that of our own industrial-based lifestyles? I began wondering some more about how industrial growth economics has served to increase the perception of separation from nature. Sitting by my own fire my state of being is partly characterised by the absence of conscious thought. When my mind is at peace I do not use it to intellectualise, to problem solve or to reason. When my mind is like this it is allowed to act in a very different way.

The evolution of the human mind has provided us with an amazing capacity for abstraction. We know the world is round and not flat, we know from Newton and his attention to scientific method that gravity was responsible for the apple falling from the tree and allegedly hitting him on the head. We know these things without direct experience of them because our mind has the ability to transcend direct experiential engagement. This is the problem with economics. It is a mathematical abstraction.

Unlike the direct and observable dependence on nature of the hunter-gatherers' economy, and to some degree the agriculturalists', the consumer within an industrial economy is separated from this directness. Thus goods and services are traded across the planet. The consumer can buy wine from Australia, beef from Argentina, furniture built with wood from the Amazon and be completely oblivious to the consequences of the depletion and pollution effects of their production, distribution and consumption.

The ability to reason and generalise is an evolutionary gift that has spawned a technological revolution in industrialised nations, with developments such as the worldwide web, improved food hygiene, increased and better transport links, more diverse leisure opportunities, improved medicine, scientific discoveries, healthcare and increased life expectancy, to name but a few. However, this conceptual ability does have consequences. One of the chief characteristics of growth economics is consumption. Today's consumption has moved beyond the basic needs of the hunter-gatherer to include luxury items. There are three consequences to this. The first is that abstract economics means that the cost to, and of, nature is often hidden from the consumer. The second is the inbuilt assumption that consumption and acquisition of material possessions will lead to personal happiness. The third is another, perhaps unacknowledged, assumption that happiness cannot be achieved without the continued purchase and consumption of material possessions. In this way our culture becomes increasingly committed to buying in the pursuit of happiness while being increasingly unaware of the consequences to nature of this increased consumption. Consequently, consumption undermines the environmental resource base it depends on.

This is what leads many commentators to conclude that if consumption patterns of the wealthiest countries in the world were adopted by all countries we would need several planets to sustain us. Growth economics within an industrial economy allows humans to *think* of themselves as detached and separate from nature.

3

The canoeist and the economist

I WOKE UP EARLY NEXT MORNING TO LAUNCH MY CANOE AND consciously tried to keep my mind uncluttered. However, along with the breaking of a new day an unexpected thought began to dawn on me. I wondered what Barry, Pete and Nev would think of their appearance in this book as my *alter egos*. While I wanted to acknowledge the profound effect their teaching had on me I reminded myself that the words spoken by their voices were in fact my own and they may not agree with what I had to say. Furthermore, I knew that they would insist that I, along with all their other students, should stand on my own two feet and think for myself.

If an *alter ego's* voice dominates internal conversations then there is a danger that the self becomes a slave to it. An enslaved voice is not able to think independently, speak out against injustice or challenge the *status quo* in times of need. An enslaved voice is a silent voice. I do like the creative frisson that this internal dialogue provides – there is always 'someone' to speak to, a voice to offer support and encouragement, and a springboard to test ideas. However, thoughts alone (whoever they come from) will not solve the environmental crisis. Just as students can stand in the shadow of their teachers' ideas so too can actions stand in the shadow of thoughts.

Set high in the hills above Loch Ness is the village of Abriachan. Recently a national project was established called the Millennium Forest for Scotland. It aims to restore the ancient native woodlands of Scotland felled in the last four hundred years for ship building, charcoal and various war efforts. Such reforestation projects are essential in the prevention of further loss of biodiversity because practices such as felling, burning and over-grazing have reduced Scotland's ancient pinewoods to as little as one per cent of their original cover.

The project works through community-based initiatives so that pockets of trees around the country will eventually be linked up to provide extensive forest areas characteristic of the climax tree cover following the last post-glacial period. The fascinating thing is that for the Abriachan community it is not just about restoring woodland for its own sake. Its aims are 'to help bring about significant physical restoration of our native woodland cover and to re-establish social, cultural and economic links between communities and their local woods'. At the heart of the project is the intention to promote the relationship between people and nature.

In one of their projects the forest has become an integral part of community life. In the woods children have created a series of natural sculptures, a bronze-age hut, a sheiling and bird hide. And there is more. In 1998 the local community successfully purchased Abriachan Forest after it had been put on the open market by the state sponsored agency Forest Enterprise. The community wanted to ensure that their traditional rights of access to the forest were ensured and decided to become a community landowner (these rights have now been superseded by the introduction of the Land Reform (Scotland) Act 2003 which provides a statutory right of access). In the community's words on their website:

> [we have] successfully increased the black grouse population by creating suitable habitats. We have restored wet areas beside streams so increasing the biodiversity. We have planted over 100,000 native species. Another very important aim was to create local employment. Our first employee was a part-time administrator. We now offer seasonal employment to local crofters, vacation work for our students and we have a policy of using local contractors where possible. Recently we have embarked on a programme of thinning in the commercial sector of our forest. This necessitated the purchase of several pieces of machinery. Local people have been trained to operate this equipment and this has resulted in further employment opportunities. We also employ a forest officer, a local graduate, who is involved in a variety of rangering and maintenance duties.

The community runs a forest school, provides a range of outdoor activities, and employs a crofter who carries out forest thinning, maintenance and firewood processing.

There is much to be learned from the way this community has gone about its business. Firstly, Abriachan is a good example of how a community can involve itself in grass-root activism and begin to shape its own future. Secondly, it has shown resilience by adapting to changing social, economic and environmental circumstances through the diversification of its operations. Thirdly, it provides another way of thinking about the production, distribution and consumption of goods and services. The scope of the economic transactions described in the last chapter were large-scale and global, but what this community shows is how economies can be developed that are small-scale and local. Fourthly, it is very apparent that part of the wealth of the community is dependent on the existence of the forest. In this way the economic transactions between people and nature become more direct and apparent when people can directly observe the effects of their labour – if you fell the forest the economy has no resource base. Thus biodiversity and the meeting of human needs are relational, more like it was for hunter-gatherers. Furthermore this relationship between biodiversity and needs can be expanded to create employment, just as was the case for the agriculturalist.

However, can small-scale community initiatives operate within or challenge the structures of industrial economies and their depleting and polluting effects on nature? Can communities like Abriachan be developed in other areas in a way that nurtures the relationships between people and nature without destroying the very resource base that economics depend on?

These are important questions but our modern political systems tend to suppress or ignore them. History provides lots of examples of the folly of suppressing important questions. Take for example the Polish astronomer Nicolaus Copernicus, whose astronomical observations led him to conclude the Earth was not the centre of the universe. This challenged the dominant

Christian belief that God had created the universe, putting the supposedly stationary Earth at its centre. Fearing the wrath of the Church he resisted publishing his findings (although they appeared after his death). His ideas were later elaborated by the Italian mathematician, Galileo Galilei, who advanced the theory by demonstrating that not only was the Earth not the centre of the universe but in fact it was merely one of several planets that revolved around the sun. While factually correct the theory was also sacrilegious. Unfortunately these findings coincided with the time of the Inquisition and he was tried and condemned as a heretic by the Roman Catholic Church and placed under house arrest for the rest of his life. The point here is that Copernicus and Galileo were not allowed to pursue the questions that were important to them. These questions, because they challenged the very core of societal values at that time, were suppressed.

I doubt anybody is going to place me under house arrest today or suppress the questions I want to ask about the dangers of growth economics to nature. However, there remain similarities within society then and now. What is common is that questions about the human-nature relationship are a challenge to the dominant value system. For Copernicus and Galileo the dominant value system involved religion. Nowadays the dominant value system of the industrialist epoch is the belief in consumption-based growth economics to provide for everyone's needs and wants. So if the questions people want to ask today are for example, 'Where will I find the cheapest food to buy?' or 'What car do I want to be seen in this year?' then both questions and answers operate within the dominant paradigm. However as soon as questions such as, 'What are the carbon costs of the food I buy?' or 'How much atmospheric pollution will my new car create?' there comes a point where the questions are actually a challenge to dominant consumerist values. Dominant value systems tend to support questions where the answers are found within the dominant value system, and tend to suppress questions that challenge the system itself. This is as true today as it was for Copernicus and Galileo.

It is in this sense that questions are more important than answers. It is not that answers are unimportant (they are essential) but what if people do not ask the right sorts of questions? What if, like Galileo and Copernicus, the questions they want to ask are suppressed? What if people do not know what questions to ask? Roughly speaking questions and answers either serve to reinforce the *status quo* or they seek to change it. Questions therefore are not just about philosophy: they are about power.

Although it is important to be solution-focused, it is even more important to consider the right sorts of questions. What defines 'right' in this case are questions that seek to challenge the power of growth economics and the superiority it assumes over nature.

It is comforting to know that there have been others who have wrestled with these issues. In 2006 Nicholas Stern published a seven-hundred-page document (*The economics of climate change*) that discussed the effect of climate change on the world economy. In it he states that: 'the scientific evidence is now overwhelming: climate change presents a unique challenge for economics: it is the greatest and widest-ranging market failure ever seen'. When I first started thinking about these things twenty years ago the only people who were calling for the reform of economics were environmentalists. But Stern is not the stereotypical environmentalist. Formerly a chief economist at the World Bank and professor of economics at the London School of Economics he published this report while he was chief economic advisor to the UK government. The point here is that there are signs that what has traditionally been thought of as radical, leftist and green is now entering the thinking of mainstream society. When you look at this shift in mainstream thinking it is possible to see the role that community-based initiatives such as the Abriachan Forest project might play in rethinking meta-economics. Small-scale projects like this will not in themselves solve the market's failure to protect the environment, but they do offer a glimpse of what Schumacher meant when he said that *Small is Beautiful*.

My thoughts were interrupted when I arrived at Cherry Island just outside Fort Augustus, once the site of a crannog. It was not always called Cherry Island. Its Gaelic name is Eilean Muireach (Murdoch's Island) but the local English-speaking soldiers at that time did not know this and named it after the cherry tree that grew there. This unfamiliarity with local language and custom is common throughout Scotland: map makers could neither spell nor pronounce native names. Instead they would ask local people the names of landscape features and write down the sounds heard by their uneducated ears. In this way the majestic Loch A'an in the very heart of the Cairngorms became Loch Avon.

At the end of Loch Ness I turned my canoe into the outflow of the River Oich. Fortunately there was a tail wind blowing and with my sail up I could make good progress up-river against the current. As the wind filled the sail it filled my spirits too and I was fully immersed in the moment, enjoying its simplicity and its effect on my well-being.

The feeling of elation was short-lived though as I came to

negotiate a shallow shingle rapid. The water ahead was too strong to paddle and sail against so I had to resort to another method of propulsion. Lining was not possible because the banks of the River Oich at that point are a tangled mass of trees and bushes. So I had to use the pole.

Poling involves standing towards the back of the canoe and using the pole to lever off the riverbed and push upstream against the current (see photo 7, plate section), not unlike what the punters do on the River Thames in Oxford and the Cam in Cambridge. As soon as you place your pole on the riverbed you have to feel that it is a good placement before you push, because it makes your body constantly move in and out of balance. When you push you are trying not only to produce forward momentum but steer at the same time. If you haven't got a good placement and you move to lever the canoe forwards then you are likely to fall in. The difference between being in or out of balance is fractional.

Poling is an art form and experienced polers can negotiate a passage upstream in large rapids and very strong currents. I am not one of those people. Not practising poling very often, I am more of a recreational poler. Until then I had no idea how important strong wrists were for sustained poling. Having weakened them from poling up parts of the River Ness on the first day, my wrists had become so sore that I had to stop. This became a major concern because the source of the pain was my tendons and I feared that I might have tenosynovitis. This inflammation of the sheath that surrounds the tendon is quite common among canoeists who grip paddles tightly over extended periods of time. It is an injury that often comes about through overuse and poor technique. I hold up my hand to being guilty of both of those. Mostly I was concerned about what it might mean for the completion of my journey because the only real cure is rest for several days, maybe weeks. With all the paddling miles ahead there was no doubt in my mind that tenosynovitis would mean the journey's end.

As it was a little early to look for a campsite I decided to make some upstream progress by wading the river. The cold water reached mostly up to my knees, sometimes up to my waist, but I warmed to the task. I enjoyed the physical hardship of making progress up-river. It seemed honest work and I liked how progress could be measured by the miles I accrued, even though I moved so slowly. Progress was hampered by a number of things though. Firstly the water was unusually high given the lack of recent rainfall, and I realised that I was wading up-river against a freshet. The River Oich is part of Scotland's hydro-electric scheme and the release I had to wade against provided a powerful current.

Because of the strength of the freshet I had to stay close to the riverbank, which was still lined with hazel trees. Their branches were so springy that they caught on my clothes and pinged back to catch my face. The thorns of bramble bushes tore at my clothes and exposed flesh and I felt flagellated by whips and thorns. To add spice to my progress I had to negotiate log jams and on one occasion had to wade out around a log jam in water above my waist. It worked fine until I got upstream and realised that one slip would float me into the blockage, with the current forcing me under and not over it. Submerged and entangled in trees, with my life-saving buoyancy aid still trying to float me to the surface, I would likely remain there until the freshet stopped releasing some time the next day. The consequences of slipping inspired sure footing and I was glad to move upstream away from the cold clutch of the log jam and the prospect of a watery grave.

During the ascent of the River Oich I developed paddling techniques not found in coaching handbooks. One of those was holding on to the overhanging branches of trees to pull the canoe upstream. The handle of my paddle formed a T-shape with the shaft and was useful for hooking on to branches for the same purpose. When I had to haul the laden canoe over half-submerged rocks I was reminded of people telling stories about pulling sleds over ice flows. Happily the rocks were not as big as the ice flows, and neither would I do a day's work to find I had actually gone backwards because of the current under the ice, but the physicality of the tasks seemed similar.

With the level of physical labour I wondered again why I had decided to travel up-river when there was a perfectly good canal running the length of the Great Glen. But although it would have been easier, the purpose of the journey was not about making things easy. However, neither was it about making the journey hard. More than anything I wanted to use the range of skills I had available to propel the canoe so that I could experience something of what it must have felt like for hunter-gatherers. I guess I wanted to encounter the landscape on its own terms where the minimum of human modification had taken place.

At the same time I was not seduced by the ideal of a so-called 'wilderness journey'. Had I been so I would probably have travelled to North America, where it is possible to be very remote from humanity's presence and its effects on the landscape. But Scotland does not have those vast tracts of wild land. Our landscape is much more populated and the purpose of my journey was to explore something of what is natural and cultural to Scotland. I can't even pretend that the River Oich, which provided me with so much adventure, is completely natural. The reason it was so exciting was because of the freshet, which was contained behind a dam and then released at certain times. So although the riverbed has been in existence since the last ice age the flow of water that passes over it is highly regulated by human actions.

The ultimate reason for taking the river and not the canal is best encapsulated by Bill Mason, who said in *Path of the paddle* that 'a journey by canoe along ancient waterways is a good way to rediscover our lost relationship with the natural world'. Since the Caledonian Canal is less than two hundred years old I felt that rivers offered a more ancient waterway to explore this relationship.

After a fierce day of upstream progress I set up camp on the banks of the River Oich. I had to be careful with the selection of the location because the freshet was still releasing and I noticed throughout the day that the flow had been fluctuating. If I selected a site too close to the river I may have ended up with the river invading my tent through the night. The desire to be dry was all the more appealing because after a day's wading my specialist trousers were no longer dry inside. Having had them for ten years I had intended this to be their last trip but it began to look like they would not last that long. They were full of holes and leaking like a sieve. Wet and with sore wrists I looked forward to a mug of tea and settled into my familiar campsite routine.

Schumacher's idea that *Small is Beautiful* starts from the premise that 'modern man does not experience himself as a part of nature but as an outside force destined to dominate and conquer it'. And once nature is conquered it is easy to see how the science of economics came to treat it rationally as a possession and something to be consumed. Schumacher's view is that 'it is inherent in the methodology of economics to ignore man's dependence on the natural world'. This leads him to conclude that 'one of the fateful errors of our age is the belief that the "problems of production" have been solved'. More specifically he suggests that growth economics fails to distinguish between income and capital, particularly where capital is defined as 'the irreplaceable capital that man has not made, but simply found and without which he can do nothing'. When this capital is considered to be income it is treated like any other goods or services to be consumed. The deciding factor is the price the purchaser is willing to pay. The production and distribution of goods and services at a global scale are based on the (false) belief that people are separate from nature.

The result of these transactions is that people actively engage in this belief by consuming goods and services that erode nature's capital. This illusion of separateness is aided by the power of science and technology to find ways of exploiting resources previously unavailable to less advanced technological-based economies. Thus increased economic activity combined with rapid population growth leads to greater demands for fossil fuels (coal, oil and gas). This in turn lubricates the energy needs of a growing economy to produce goods and services for distribution and consumption. In this way the cycle of perpetual growth continues to escalate.

A lot of people now recognise what Schumacher was saying and do indeed believe that nature's capital is being depleted and polluted. People who buy organic food and Fairtrade products, or who cycle to work and carbon offset their flights, are all trying to adopt a lifestyle that acts out these beliefs. Indeed these are all laudable examples of people living their lives consciously aware of the problem of production and trying in their own way to make a difference through consumption patterns. However, the illusion that Schumacher talks of is not just about individuals. It is something more systemic and overarching, something that blinds governments and social institutions to the problems of production.

Growth economics is so powerful that paradoxically its forces become almost invisible to us in our everyday lives. Thus we do not always see the consequences of our actions when we consume. Yet growth economics is responsible for the depletion of resources and for much pollution on the planet.

Waiting for the water to boil these sorts of ideas circulated around my head only to prick my conscience. Who am I to comment on other people's lifestyles when my own is far from perfect? What right does a canoeist have to talk about economics?

Perhaps what matters is that I am a person living on this planet, right now, with problems on my mind. If I were a road digger, dentist, farmer, computer technician, forestry manager, scientist, conservationist or developer the questions I had about our relationship with nature and the consequences of these relationships would still matter.

If growth economics is part of the problem then it is not for an expert economist to lecture anyone on what they do or do not know, because the problem is not so much of economics but its purpose. Do we want to live in the *status quo* where the environment serves economics (the current position) or develop another system where economics serves the environment? Experts or not, if people do not speak out then we become locked in the mindset that created the problem in the first place and end up being part of the problem we have identified.

This is what Schumacher meant when he added to the title of

his book *Small is Beautiful* the subtitle *A Study of Economics as if People Mattered*.

Jonathon Porritt followed up these ideas in a book called *Capitalism as if the World Matters*. I pointed out earlier that the economic transactions between people and nature are relational; Porritt develops this idea by suggesting that this relationship is complicated by two potentially contradictory imperatives.

> [T]he first is a biological imperative: to learn to live sustainably on this planet. This is an *absolute* imperative in that it is determined by the laws of nature and, hence, is non-negotiable – this side of extinction it permits no choice. The second is a political imperative: to aspire to improve our material standard of living year on year. This is a *relative* imperative in that it is politically determined, with a number of alternative economic paradigms available to us.

It is good news for this canoeist to hear that there are alternative economic paradigms – maybe there is some hope for nature and ourselves as a species yet. Also the distinction between absolute and relative needs is important because it helps to distinguish between needs and wants. Furthermore, it goes right to the heart of the problem of sustainability, which is to do with the nature of the human condition. Growth economics has been a spectacular success because it has identified this human condition and exploited it. The condition known to us all is self-interest.

Self-interest is evident throughout our history. It is articulated most powerfully in the Age of Enlightenment, which gave birth to its key concept of 'progress', in which societies and individuals worked hard to better themselves in the belief that the future can always be better than the present. It is not surprising to note that the Age of Enlightenment corresponds directly with the industrialist epoch and the development of growth economics. Before this, hunter-gathers and to a lesser extent agriculturalists were more preoccupied with absolute than relative needs. This is a good indication that relative needs are not a precondition of human life. This is not to say that had the opportunities available to us today been available to previous epochs they would not have behaved in similar consumptive patterns as ourselves. Consequently it is pointless to suggest that the problems caused by industry, and the concomitant consequences of depletion and pollution, can be solved by returning to a hunter-gatherer or agriculturalist lifestyle. It is more realistic to suggest that solutions to sustainable living may be found by addressing self-interest.

Acknowledging the self-interest aspect of the human condition is central to understanding why many people know that there is a problem with consumer lifestyles yet continue with those lifestyles anyway. It also raises the question of whether consumer culture brings the satisfaction that nurtures our happiness, health, well-being and prosperity. Put another way, the belief that happiness, health, well-being and prosperity comes from consumption is nothing but *post-hoc* rationalisation – a justification for the present economic system. Consequently, any solution to Schumacher's 'problems of production' must begin by linking human needs with the capacity of nature to sustain us. Furthermore, rather than assuming that our needs can be met through present consumption patterns, why not return to the question of 'what makes us happy?' and see where that takes us? This way the canoeist gets to set the questions and the economist can help to answer them.

However the canoeist needs to tread very carefully because the economist knows that the human condition of self-interest fuels growth economics, and so society by its collective nature embraces the system. The problem is that unrestrained self-interest is likely to lead to a 'business as usual' approach where growth economics continues unabated and GDP remains the measurement of satisfaction. Meantime nature's capital continues to be depleted and polluted. The problem with self-interest is that it is such a powerful motivating force there is no point in fighting it but to recognise it, harness it, and if possible redirect it.

In short we need a moral economy. The idea of a moral economy can be traced back to Adam Smith, the Scottish moral philosopher. Smith was one of the key figures of the Scottish Enlightenment and is often referred to as the father of economics. The theory of economics was based on the belief that self-interest and competition could lead to happiness, health, well-being and prosperity. At first glance Smith may seem to be the villain of the piece, someone whose theory of economics has been responsible for the depletion and pollution of nature. This is not quite true because, as Porritt says, what Smith meant was that 'self-interest has to be pursued by people of conscience, informed by their capacity for moral awareness'.

When Smith was developing his theory of economics it was still the early years of the industrialist epoch. He could never have foreseen the effect that population growth and high levels of economic activity, fuelled by astonishing advances in science and technology, would have on nature some two hundred years later. If he had maybe he would have gone somewhere to think. Perhaps he'd have chosen to go *Canoeing around the Cairngorms* and worked out another theory instead. He has, however, left an important legacy – that morals are central to economic activity, something conspicuously absent in the twenty-first century. This is not evident in modern society, where you can buy what you want without having to think of the consequences. For example, the numbers of certain species of fish are at a critical level yet they are still traded on the open market. Consumers who buy such species from fishmongers, supermarkets and fish and chip shops will not necessarily know how overfishing has caused the collapse of Canada's Atlantic fisheries and how communities have struggled as a result. In the North Sea the numbers of several species are at a critical level and yet various European countries continue to fish without allowing the depleted stocks to recover. Without awareness between cause and consequence there remains an inherent assumption within growth economics that buying is 'moral free'.

The point is that the moral fabric of society into which Smith's economics was born has changed and it is time to reconsider the nature of economics and morals. If Adam Smith had been with me in my canoe I would have asked him what a moral framework might look like that could provide the inspiration for a system of modern economics equipped to deal with the issues of depletion, pollution and social justice. I would like to have asked him what values it would be based on if such a system were developed today.

Since he was not around to consult I refer again to one of today's leading thinkers in search of answers. Jonathon Porritt is a former teacher, former chair of the UK Green Party and Director of Friends of the Earth, co-founder of the sustainable development charity Forum for the Future and chair of the UK government's independent advisory board the Sustainable Development Commission. He suggests that economics should be based on values that are determined by knowing that the future of the human species is bound by the planet's ability to sustain us.

The problem though is how to change economic theory so that it is informed by such values and principles. The challenge is for consumer choices to move from 'consequence ignorant' to 'consequence aware'. However, this will require some degree of motivation on the part of consumers.

Here Porritt may well provide the beginnings of an answer. He uses a quote from environmental philosopher Fritjof Capra to make his point.

Ultimately, deep ecological awareness is spiritual... When the concept of the human spirit is understood as the mode of consciousness in which the individual feels a sense of belonging, of connectedness, to the cosmos as a whole, it becomes clear that ecological awareness is spiritual in its deepest sense.

Here is a government advisor talking about an economic framework that has at its source spirituality. In one sense this is not all that bizarre because Adam Smith's moral framework also celebrated the spirit in the form of self-interest (and how that self-interest benefited communities and society). But Porritt and Capra are suggesting something else here. They are suggesting that self-interest can be nurtured in order to lessen human impact on the natural world, and that spirituality is central to this process.

This makes theoretical sense but the problem is that Porritt does not say what the essence of this spirituality is nor how it can be nurtured, a crucial point if it is to be part of the formulation of a moral framework for economics. Here I think the canoeist has something to say to the economist.

First, it is important to note the medium of communication being used when we share ideas about spirituality. When Porritt reads Capra, and I read Porritt and when you read this the mode of communication is the written word. We are therefore talking about spirituality from a rational and theoretical perspective.

If we look at the passage of time from the hunter-gatherer through to the agriculturalist through to the industrialist, we note that there has been a gradual move from outdoors to indoors. With that move it is easy to see how people can forget the connectedness that Capra and Porritt speak of. The Age of Reason and its almost God-like celebration of the mind simply deprioritises the embodied nature-based experiences of our hunter-gatherer ancestors while simultaneously intellectualising spirituality. It is possible therefore that one of the problems with thinking up a new moral framework is that it depends too much on thinking about it.

If Capra and Porritt are right about spirituality being core to the relationship between people and nature then surely rationality is part of the problem. Rationality allows us to separate subjects from objects, mind from body and ultimately people from planet. I am not suggesting that rationality has no place. But if part of this moral framework is to do with the connectedness of people and nature, and if this connectedness has a spiritual dimension that is metaphysical, then it would appear that how we experience nature is profoundly important to the way we end up thinking about 'it'.

It has been a hard slog ascending the River Oich, both physically and mentally. The final obstacle I had to overcome was a weir where the river flows out of Loch Oich. It was too steep to paddle, pole or line and so from the bank I hauled the canoe by a painter and then settled down for lunch beside a sign that said, 'It is dangerous to cross this weir in a canoe'. A sign should be erected beside it that says, 'It is dangerous for canoeists not to think about economics'. But I am comforted in the knowledge that communities like Abriachan provide other ways of thinking about economics and our relationship with nature. I think this is what Schumacher had in mind when he said that *Small is Beautiful*.

4

Time and cycles

Loch Oich is only eight kilometres long but my progress along it was slow. In the middle of the loch a headwind of between force four and five was blowing. By staying close to the shore I was able to take shelter from the worst of it but I still had to be as efficient with the use of my energy as possible.

The constant search for the 'sweet-spot' has its origins in Newton's Third Law of Motion which states that 'for every action there is an equal and opposite reaction'. In calm conditions the canoe will sit steady in the water, but this absence of motion changes when other forces are considered. The wind moves the canoe in much the same way as it affects a weathercock. If my canoe is unladen and I sit at the back then my weight lightens the front. If the wind happens to be a headwind it will use my body weight as an axis point and spin the lighter front end around 180 degrees and point me in the wrong direction. To compensate I can use the laws of physics to my advantage. I can shift the axis point by moving my body weight forward in the canoe to find the 'sweet-spot', where the force of the wind no longer spins me round but holds me steady, pointing into it. I can also use the weight of my equipment to adjust the axis point. This movement of body and equipment is known as 'trimming' the canoe. With the weight well forward I have the optimal trim to make progress.

After adjusting the trim fore and aft I also needed to attend to the canoe's lateral dimensions. Moving my weight to one side of the canoe does two things. The first is that the canoe moves from a stable position known as 'primary stability' through a position of relative instability, before arriving at a point of 'secondary stability' where the chine of the canoe sits deep in the water. By maintaining balance the practiced canoeist can move through the point of instability with ease. However, the movement is often the precursor to a capsize for novices because the idea of getting the gunnel closer to the water to make the canoe stable seems counter-intuitive and often leads to overcompensation, and a soaking. A second thing results from shortening the distance between the gunnel and the water. With the canoe edged on to its side the paddle can go deeper in the water and the canoeist gets more leverage to power against the strong wind. This is where my red cherry paddle functions at its best. It digs deep into the water and I can power forwards, ready to steer the canoe when I retrieve. Thus I made progress up the loch, using these skills to weave my way between the shore and a beautiful tree-clad island. In a landscape characterised by deforestation, the island is an oasis of biodiversity. Protected first from loggers and now from the grazing of sheep and deer, its relative inaccessibility has proved to be its salvation from both two- and four-legged predators.

The main geological fault lines in Scotland lie on a south-west to north-east orientation. As I noted earlier the Great Glen fault line along which I journeyed is one of these. It connects the town of Fort William in the south-west with Inverness in the north-east. Its deep trench is filled by a chain of lochs and connecting rivers. It is known to be the most seismically active tear fault (so called because its rocky plates move sideways against one another) in Britain, with over sixty tremors in the last two hundred years.

Hauled up on the side of Loch Oich, surrounded by hills, lunch at hand, I looked around to immerse myself in the landscape. It was fashioned first by this seismic activity. Then, during the last ice age, rivers of ice followed the natural line of least resistance, inheriting the existing valley, deepening and widening it as it went. A huge glacier scoured the trench, which accounts for the steep smooth flanks of the hillside above and the deep chasm below the water surface.

The evidence of the glacier's passing is there to see in the striations, or scratches, they leave behind on the rock. The striations were scored on the hills' flanks when the glacier picked up rocks that then became embedded in the ice. Those rocks that protruded from the ice scoured the valley floors and walls with the movement of the glacier. The passage of the glacier also left behind a classic example of a U-shaped valley. Standing and looking at this history written into the landscape it is hard not to be impressed by these immense forces of nature. Such traces on the landscape provide a context for human existence. They help to convey a sense of presence and absence, of time and space.

And that explains why I kept slowing the journey down. When I did there was a sense of the present around me and the beautiful mountains filled my spirits. Yet simultaneously it was a reminder that I was gazing over a history archive. The landscape seemed like a window into the past.

Nev introduced me to rocks in my first ever lesson about landscape. There are three basic rock types. Igneous rocks form from the cooling of liquid magma. If the magma cools before breaking the surface the resulting rock is called intrusive. If the magma breaks the surface, as happens in a volcano, it becomes known as lava. Once on the surface it cools and is called extrusive rock. Sedimentary rocks are so called because they are composed of loose sediments. These sediments are fragments of rocks and minerals, or animal and plant materials, which take an incredible journey as they are washed downstream to settle in layers in rivers, lakes, seas and oceans. Once settled they are then compacted together and over time form layer upon layer of rock. Metamorphic rocks form beneath the Earth's surface. These were once igneous or sedimentary rocks and have since gone through a process of change as a result of the increase in heat and pressure which transforms them into more compact rocks.

While categorising rocks into these three main types is a helpful way of identifying them and giving them a name, what is almost beyond imagination is that they are not and never have been in a state of permanence. Often credited as being the founding father of geology, the Scottish scientist James Hutton showed how all three rock types were inter-related through a rock cycle. One entry point into the cycle is when igneous rocks from hot magma solidifies. Then, in the words of the *Concise Encyclopedia Earth*:

> when exposed on the Earth's surface, these rocks are worn down by weathering and erosion into tiny

fragments. Wind and water carry the fragments to the sea, where they settle in layers on the seabed. They slowly turn into sedimentary rocks as they are buried deeper. These rocks are either worn away to form new sedimentary rocks, or are transformed by pressure and heat into metamorphic rocks. Exposed metamorphic rocks are in turn worn away to form new sedimentary rock.

The cycle is completed when magma rises from the Earth's mantle through metamorphic and sedimentary layers, melting the surrounding rock to form new igneous rock. Furthermore, the mighty forces of tectonic plates as they collide, fold and mountain build have their own effect on the evolution of new rock.

The landscape around Loch Oich is characterised by movement and impermanence which is often not apparent at first sight. One of the wonders of the modern age, the World Wide Web, provides excellent sites that have interactive rock cycle animations. These help to explain something that is difficult to comprehend to the eye conditioned to think of mountains as immovable and immutable objects: the powers of nature that transform the landscape and write history into the rocks.

My efforts to make headway into a force five wind was a reminder of the incredible forces of nature that shaped the landscape around me. I felt humbled and chastised that the idea of 'conquering' this amazing landscape might ever have entered my mind. Standing at the edge of the loch I found it hard to think of myself as some distant observer – I sensed some understanding of geological deep time and that I was very much part of the landscape, but I struggled to find words to explain the feelings. I was reminded of a saying that Pete is fond of making: 'We are but small people in a very big landscape.'

Through understanding places, and travelling through them as slowly as I have, we can build relationships with landscape. The more we come to know, the stronger the relationship. This is different from just reading about landscapes from a book. Sure, I have read books to learn about these things, but the knowledge I refer to is more than just theoretical – it is filled with feeling. It is not unlike relationships between people. We don't learn to love a spouse, parent, daughter, son or sibling by reading about them. To make the relationship grow and last we have to work at it, nurture it in times of trouble, find out more about the other, even when we thought we knew the other well enough already.

On the west side of Loch Oich stands an obelisk-shaped monument. In the seventeenth century two members of the Clan McDonnell were murdered by seven assailants. The chief of the clan took his revenge by sending a band of his own henchmen who executed all seven, removed their heads and took them back to McDonnell as proof that the deed had been done. On the way the leader of the band stopped to wash blood from the heads to make them more presentable to his clan chief. After this incident the spot became known as the Well of the Seven Heads. Visitors are provided with a graphic reminder of these events – on the top of the obelisk you can see a sculpture of the seven heads and a hand holding a dagger. I was happy to move on from this place of evil deeds, though stories like this are important. Without them you can't know the landscape.

Loch Oich and Loch Lochy are linked by the Caledonian Canal. The highest point of the Great Glen waterway is between these two points so once I had crossed that watershed it would be 'downhill' all the way to the west coast. I had already decided not to use the canal and so I loaded my canoe onto the trolley I had with me and began a three-kilometre portage along the towpath that links the lochs. Using the canal would be much easier, but for the same reasons I canoed *up* the rivers Ness and Oich I wanted to experience the Great Glen as close as possible to the way my ancestors experienced it.

My chosen option meant unloading the canoe, reloading it on to a trolley, dragging it and then reloading on to the water at the other end of the portage. Despite the ancestor argument it might still not be evident why I took a more 'difficult' option when there was a much 'easier' option. This only holds up when 'difficult' is associated with bad and 'easy' is associated with good. The environmental problems around the industrialised world have been caused by consumption patterns of the majority who avoid difficult lifestyle choices by taking easy and preferable options.

In addition to the physical element, this journey was also meant to be a metaphor for how we live life in a particular way. Perhaps the idea that continually travelling downstream, the easy, so-called, 'progressive way', is part of the problem. Perhaps by canoeing uphill the scenery from that direction would provide new ways of thinking about the relationship between people and nature. So the journey was not about making things harder: it was simply trying to seek solutions by looking at things in different ways, to challenge the limitations of easy ways and discover if the difficult ways really are that difficult.

Besides, had I taken the easy option and canoed along the canal I would not have had an encounter with a family on the towpath. They asked jovially why I was taking my canoe for a walk. I explained about my environmental concerns, the history of the voyageurs and how this was once a hunting craft that trappers would use to portage equipment and furs. The father good-humouredly suggested that I was unlikely to find good quality pelts around here. Looking at his scalp I cheekily said, 'You'd better watch yourself then.' He rubbed his bald head, smiled and said, 'You'll not get much money for mine.'

We went our separate ways and I wondered what impression I had left. Is someone dragging a canoe along a path on a day when the sun is beating down to be taken seriously? What with the heat and self-doubt I thought I was hallucinating when I walked around a corner of the towpath and encountered a sign saying 'Pub' on top of a barge. As I drew near I saw that there was nobody around and I thought it a cruel hoax left over from April Fools' Day. So I was pleasantly surprised when the landlord peered out to enquire if the guy taking his canoe for a walk was thirsty. The barge pub sold real ale and once inside and chatting with others I thought the place to be the source of all knowledge. An hour or so later, with 'well-being' coursing through my veins, any self-doubt was replaced by feeling completely at one with nature. I paddled into Loch Lochy towards the fading sun to find somewhere to camp.

Travelling east to west means that around midday you dissect the sun's parabola at right angles, which has important consequences for camping between high-sided mountains. If you camp on the northern bank of the loch the setting sun drops behind the hillside, shielding you from its warm glow, meaning a cold campsite. However, in the morning the benefit is having the early morning sun rising over the opposite side and warming your campsite as you get out of your sleeping bag. If, on the other hand, you camp on the southern side of the loch then you get the opposite effect. There was a high-pressure weather system overhead and so I expected a morning frost. I opted for camping on the colder northern side in order to enjoy the warmth of the early sun – for three mornings I had woken to minus temperatures and had to pull on socks and boots that, wet from wading up the rivers, had frozen overnight. The thought of pulling on wet but not frozen socks first thing in the morning seemed almost pleasurable.

By the time I had the tent set up the sun had already dropped behind the hills called Meall na Teanga (Hill of the Tongue) and Sron a' Choire Ghairbh (Nose of the Rough Corrie). Their Gaelic names are poetic reminders of the past when Gaels would have gazed upon these same hills, noting the resemblance of their topography to human features and naming them accordingly. I had stopped here once before and feel a strong affiliation with the place because of the experiences I shared with Jane. We had walked up Meall na Teanga in very wet and windy conditions. In such conditions it would have been prudent to have aborted our ascent; however, I was determined to get to the top of another Munro. Normally when we walk together Jane does a lot of talking and I do a lot of listening. On this day though, being wet and chilled to the bone, there was no chattering. My predilection for gentle teasing together with a desire to walk, often without conversation, led me to rename Meall na Teanga as The Silence of the Tongue.

With pleasant memories of landscape and people offering some inner warmth I went in search of firewood for another sort of heat. Foraging for firewood must be one of the few modern-day activities that brings us close to the lifestyle of our hunter-gatherer ancestors. It is therapeutic to be engaged in a simple physical exercise that brings a tangible reward almost instantly. For the hunter-gatherer foraging was born of necessity, but I wonder too what forms of well-being they experienced as they went about their tasks. I wonder also if people nowadays could find more pleasure in simple tasks that did not involve such a carbon-dependent lifestyle.

With a fire burning it is natural to think of carbon. The flames burn brightly when fanned by the wind; they recede as they consume the very wood that keeps them alive and so there is a need to put more wood on. I imagined our hunter-gatherer ancestors gorged with cooked meat sitting around fires chatting, staring and contemplating. No doubt the content and context of these thoughts have changed as hunter-gatherers became agriculturalists who then became industrialists, but surely there would have been some commonality that links people's thoughts throughout the ages. When you sit around a fire your mind is free to look into it for wisdom. While this can be a profoundly spiritual engagement it is also a scientific enquiry. Carbon is one source of an elemental and eternal truth.

Just as I have little formal training as an economist so I have had not much as a scientist. What I do know is that books, the internet and other people can help understand scientific ideas if there is sufficient curiosity in the first place.

Carbon comes from the Latin *carbo* and means coal. Hunter-gatherers knew about carbon. They may not have articulated it using the written word, as I am doing now, but they would have articulated it through practical activity in their daily lives by manufacturing charcoal for their fires. Just as carbon showed up in their lives it shows up in ours. Because of its unusual ability to bond with itself and a range of other elements, carbon is found everywhere on the Earth. It is found in the atmosphere as carbon dioxide. It is found in rocks such as the calcium carbonates that make up limestone, and it is found dissolved in fresh and salt water. It is in the 'lead' used in pencils, the diamonds that adorn fingers, wrists and necks; it is also in clothes, food and the air we breathe. It is present in all life forms. Around one fifth of the mass of the adult human body is made up of carbon and it is also part of our DNA structure.

This means that carbon is both inorganic (something traditionally considered to be non-living and of mineral origin) and organic (something traditionally considered to be living and of biological origin). Carbon is a reminder that although matter can be separated and described in this way the differences are often celebrated more than the commonalities. To separate things into living and non-living denies the underlying reality that carbon is common and a precursor to the existence of both.

Looking into a fire is to consider evolutionary time. It helps to provide the pauses between thoughts, to contemplate learning. Although theoretical learning is important, in fact essential, direct experiences of phenomena is a powerful stimulant to learn. Pete taught me this; he likes fires. As a scientist he knows that if people understand carbon then they will understand a lot about life.

As with the 'rock cycle', scientists describe the 'carbon cycle', and here photosynthesis is as good a place to start as any. Photosynthesis, as McKean and Jones say in their *Introduction to human and social biology*, is 'the production of food by a green plant from carbon dioxide and water using the energy from sunlight which is trapped by chlorophyll'. One of the consequences of photosynthesis is the production of oxygen: without plants converting water and carbon dioxide into glucose and oxygen, we would have no oxygen to breathe, and indeed would not have evolved. In other words all life on Earth depends on the process of photosynthesis.

As plants photosynthesise they remove carbon in the form of carbon dioxide from the atmosphere and store it in their structure. Carbon is also important in the development of animal tissue as it is absorbed by herbivores from the plants that they eat, and by carnivores eating other animals that have ingested carbon-filled plants. When organisms respire, die, and decay, carbon is released back into the atmosphere. The oceans too are included in the cycle. Carbon is exchanged from the atmosphere to the ocean through diffusion and the carbon ends up dissolved in seawater. Shellfish use this carbon in the production of their shells. When these organisms die their shells sink to the ocean floor where they accumulate and begin the process of transformation into sedimentary rock. In this way carbon cycles around the planet as it is exchanged between its four major reservoirs: the atmosphere, biosphere, hydrosphere and lithosphere.

Remarkably, the carbon liberated from the fire I was sitting in front of was once part of the atmosphere. In the process of burning it was being returned to the atmosphere following a period of temporary storage in wood. Even more remarkable is that the transformation of carbon into sedimentary rocks means that the carbon and rock cycles are part of an even bigger cycle. It is possible to imagine carbon and rock cycling through time and space on an eternal journey. Learning more about the Earth's cycles is central to understanding the relationship between people and nature.

The time the carbon spent stored in that wood was only a temporary part of its cycle. To understand that is to understand a little more about deep time. The body that I call 'me' is a collection of molecules and elements that have temporarily come together to form a human individual whose current ambition is to *Canoe around the Cairngorms*. In another half a lifetime or so this organism will, like the wood smoke before me, begin the process of decay, releasing the molecules and elements to continue their ceaseless cycle. When looked at in this way what I call 'me' has only a temporary existence.

I do not mean to demean human individuality but rather to celebrate it. For all of the cycles that contribute to life and for all the evolutionary twists and turns of extinctions, we all exist as a function of nature's creation. Those of a religious persuasion may well interpret the idea of this blessing differently from those of a secular persuasion, but if you believe in the truth of the cycles then there is one conclusion to be drawn. The Earth operates as a complex system of cycles and human beings are part of those cycles. Nature is omnipotent and omnipresent. This planet that sustains us is part of us and we are part of it. The truth of this is written in every rock, plant and animal that we pass on our own journeys. It is written into the invisible air that we breathe and the water that kept my canoe afloat.

Perhaps the last word on this idea of planetary interconnection should be left to the scientist James Lovelock, famous for his development of Gaia theory. He said, 'Evolution is not just a property of organisms – what evolves is the whole Earth system with its living and non-living parts existing as a tight coupled entity.'

5

Me and my shadow

I WOKE TO THE PROMISE OF ANOTHER BRIGHT AND DRY DAY. It was still too early for the sun to show itself and once again I faced the prospect of pulling on frozen socks. I considered a treat in order and allowed them to thaw over the warmth of the stove.

My plan for the day was to reach the River Lochy, after which it would be downhill all the way to Loch Linnhe and the sea. However, a headwind blowing at least force five was to have a greater say in proceedings than my own ambitions. Inevitably a build-up of lactic acid in my muscles meant that I had to switch from left to right to ease the pain of prolonged exercise and test my bilateral competency. As I powered forwards it was essential to maintain concentration in the retrieve phase to ensure accurate steering. Letting the nose go even a fraction either side of the 'sweet-spot' would mean the wind catching enough of the canoe to turn it round, whereupon the canoe would stall and be blown swiftly in the opposite direction. Even a slight movement to relieve pressure on a cramped leg muscle can be enough to alter the trim, move the axis or change the shape of the chine in the water and lose the 'sweet-spot'. The level of concentration required is physically demanding and psychologically wearing.

With the wind forcing me backwards it was not the time for philosophising and I decided to land and wait for the wind to drop. Wind is rarely steady in its strength. Sometimes it is just a case of waiting until the gusts peak and drop off, and making some progress before they strengthen again. However standing around waiting for a lull just led to impatience and it was not long before I was back in my canoe making progress by poling the canoe near to the shore. Greater power is provided from levering the pole off the loch bed than from powering the paddle through the water.

Just as on the river, as soon as you place your pole on a loch bed you have to feel that it is a good placement before you push on it. Moving your balance point can easily result in a capsize. In these conditions the four factors that need to be considered are your bodyweight distribution, the trim of the canoe, wind strength and direction, and skilful pole use. If you were to stand on dry land and lean ever further forwards or backwards, or to one side, then at some point you would fall over. With a pole in your hand you could prevent this happening by leaning on it. This is what happens when you are poling and it all becomes a little more complicated when you factor in the wind and the movement of the canoe over water, not to mention the fear of falling in.

Within this fine balance point you then have to transfer power from the body to the pole to provide both forward momentum and steerage. Even in calm conditions if you get a loose placement it is easy to fall overboard. To fall overboard in these conditions, and assuming the canoe did not capsize, would mean it and me parting company at an alarming rate. The canoe would be blown away down the loch and I would be left with a cold swim to the side. I would then have to spend the rest of the day trying to retrieve the canoe from wherever it landed. Poling is therefore an art that is wise to master.

Further complications arise when you move from poling to paddling. At the point where you decide that your paddling efforts are making no headway and you decide to pole instead you have to move quickly. From a kneeling position your last paddle stroke is important because it provides power and steerage into the wind. With your pole already assembled it is then 'just' a case of grabbing it, standing up, adjusting the trim through body movement, maintaining the angle into the wind and keeping the canoe moving without stalling. When it works well no forward momentum is lost and the whole movement feels seamless.

Poling was tiring though, and with my wrists sore I landed regularly to line the canoe from the bank. To line the canoe in those conditions all I needed to do was allow the wind coming from directly ahead to push the nose of the canoe out into the water, just as the current of the river had. If the front of the canoe was set at an angle of around thirty degrees into the wind then so long as I maintained it using my lines the rest was fairly straightforward. The system worked well until a tree or bush threatened to tangle the ropes, at which point I had to either walk round it, wade, pole, paddle or stop for a rest.

Loch Lochy is only around eighteen kilometres long, five of which I paddled on my first day on the loch. Another day of strong winds meant that I reached the south-western end with relief: there it opened out and another valley joined from the west. As often happens when valleys meet the wind direction changed and instead of a headwind I had a quartering wind pushing at me from the side. Counting my blessings I adjusted the trim to compensate for the change and relished the prospect of sailing the last three kilometres to the mouth of the River Lochy.

This three kilometres was the first test of my new sail in a strong wind. The sailing rig was cleverly designed, with the sail itself rectangular and measuring one hundred and ten by one hundred and sixty centimetres. My poling pole split into two. Half the pole acted as a mast while the other half inserted diagonally through a sleeve in the sail and acted as a boom to provide support. One of the canoe thwarts had been drilled to allow the mast to pass through. The foot of the mast then sat in a mast step glued onto the canoe bottom. Quite a robust system – at least I had thought so.

At first I was pleased with its performance. It took a lot of pressure as I moved the stern through the eye of the wind, jibing from side to side. The force from the sail made the canoe lean heavily so I had to use my bodyweight to lean into the wind as a counterbalance. In that rather precarious position I had a bit of a fright when the mast step broke loose, leaving the canoe on the brink of a capsize. The canoe began bucking, with the loosely secured sail intermittently filling and deflating as the wind's energy transferred to the canoe in sudden jolts. I had tied the rope around a thwart on a quick release knot, which I pulled to let the wind out of the sail. No sooner had I done that than the unsecured sail began flapping madly. The loose rope cracked like a whip around my head. How could this happen in the relative safety of a small inland loch? If the canoe were to capsize I would have at least a kilometre to swim to the bank, plus the indignity of needing someone to rescue my canoe from the water. 'Never underestimate open water, however small it is,' I heard my own voice say, just as I would have lectured beginner canoeists who, because they have coped with paddling white-water rapids, thought they had nothing to fear from the so-called 'flat water' of a loch. I was lucky this time and succeeded in bringing the sail down before it broke the thwart, whipped or capsized me.

Licking my wounds I headed into the narrowing at the south end of the loch, where it was increasingly sheltered from the wind, and counted myself lucky to be still on course. It wasn't long, though, before a sense of mischief replaced the feeling of foreboding as I noticed a salmon farm ahead. I canoed over a floating boom then moved from cage to cage watching these creatures leap and felt a wave of nostalgia wash over me. Since childhood I have been fascinated with fish and water. My grandparents would take my brother, sister and me on fishing holidays and the memories of these trips remain vivid. The eastern seaboard fishing towns of Arbroath, Buckie, and Cullen were favourites and so too were villages on the north side of the Moray Firth such as Balintore and Portmahomack. These holidays also included fishing the rivers and lochs in Sutherland, Ross-shire and Inverness-shire. These were all places where I learned to tie knots, undo tangles and sometimes catch fish, but more importantly I began a love affair with wild places.

What I did not know at the time was that all of those experiences were to prove formative. Sigurd Olsen in *Listening point* says that 'while we are born with curiosity and wonder and our early years full of the adventure they bring, I know such inherent joys are often lost'. I think I know what he means. The industrialist way of life provides a barrier that insulates people from nature and it is easy for those inherent joys to be lost as people spend more of their time in the digital world. I know because I am one of those people who spends too much time in a job dominated by email communication and bureaucratic administration procedures. Olsen also offers hope because these formative experiences and inherent joys do not disappear, they are only hiding, saying 'their latent glow can be fanned to flame again'. To see a fish leap tears away the artificial veils of civilisation and fans the flames of those formative elemental experiences. I felt the latent glow that Olsen speaks of.

But it is not necessarily that simple. The relationship between humanity and nature will not be improved simply because young people have nature-based experiences that turn out to be formative. I know this because nowadays rationality and emotion combine to provide a confusing reality for me. When I watched those magnificent, lithe spears of pure muscle I imagined them being on the end of my line and the fun I'd have playing them into the landing net. That was certainly what I dreamed of as a boy. Catching your first salmon was a rite of passage and I remember mine with great clarity. I was twelve and I can picture the favourite inlet I would always head for, the stone I stood beside, the birch trees I stood among and the heather-clad hills that surrounded the loch. I remember how overcast the day was, how fearful I was that the salmon would get away and no-one would believe I had it on the line. I remember too the first people I spoke to about it and how proud my mother was. Today I still like to fish, but my mind plays tricks on me. The innocence of catching my first salmon is often replaced by the guilt of causing pain. I can counter-rationalise this emotion by saying I am going to eat whatever I catch, or that fish do not feel pain in the same way that mammals do. But it's not that simple. Fish do feel pain. I have tried fishing with a fly that has no hook but it is totally unsatisfactory because I know that I cannot catch fish, which is what the predator in me really wants to do. I have tried returning them live to the water but can't convince myself that terrorising them and letting them go is any better than killing them.

This tension between what I feel and what I think I call my Shadow Self. The idea comes from the theory developed by the Swiss psychiatrist Carl Jung, who argued not only that everyone has a Shadow Self but, more importantly, that to ignore it is unhealthy. So although fishing may be a tension in my life the answer is not to try to bury the tension but pay attention to it. Even though I can't fully explain why the tension exists, to ignore it is to ignore a powerful voice trying to tell me something.

Allowing the Shadow Self to reveal itself is an important precondition to understanding our relationship with nature. To suppress our Shadow Self is to ignore something that we already suspect but fail to address for fear that it will affect our lifestyles. For example, ignoring the Shadow Self allows us to ignore the welfare of animals before they end up as meat on our dinner plates. It allows us to ignore the mountains of waste we create that end up incinerated or in landfills. It allows us to exploit cheap air fares knowing that there are associated pollution costs. It is easy to externalise these problems as someone else's and say, for example, 'It's up to the government to sort that out.'

When the Shadow Self is ignored or suppressed we live in denial of our own individual problems. As Jung says, it is unhealthy, not just for us, but for the other species whose welfare we ignore. So the tensions inherent in the Shadow Self are to be welcomed for what they tell us about ourselves both individually and collectively. Jung would say that ignoring the Shadow Self is the reason that smokers continue to smoke despite knowing that it is bad for them, why alcoholics drink more than is good for them, and why obese people eat more than is healthy. Context is essential and nature-based experiences provide first-hand opportunities to inform that voice. Like any other voice the Shadow Self sounds louder the closer you get to its source.

Industrial society has become very good at ignoring the Shadow Self and humanity's connection with nature. The salmon I saw jumping around inside cages are not really 'magnificent, lithe spears of pure muscle', a description that was a figment of my imagination as I recalled the wild salmon of my youth. Those wild salmon would have streaked through the seas off the west coast of Greenland in pursuit of herring, sand eels and shrimps, and would themselves have been preyed upon by seals. On their return to fresh water, driven by a powerful homing instinct incomprehensible to the human mind, they have to leap up waterfalls to reach their spawning grounds. All the time their muscles are being honed through incredible feats of speed and endurance. These are the fish I had in mind.

The fish in cages circle relentlessly around their pens. Food is delivered to their mouths; there is no chase involved. Routine and captivity dominate their lives. Whether wild or farmed, salmon require a high-protein diet. Because of this the dietary requirements of wild fish have to be mimicked by fish farmers. These creatures have been fed on pellets of food made up from the minced remains of fish including offal. 'Small Fish' fishing is part of a separate industry known as 'feed fisheries' and takes place in both the Southern and Northern hemispheres. So not only are environmental impacts of salmon farming local they are also global in the sense that the sustainability of the individual species of 'Small Fish' is uncertain. Add to that the fossil fuel consumption in transporting the salmon feed to Scotland and it becomes apparent that the environmental impact of salmon farming has consequences well beyond these Scottish shores.

On top of this salmon and other species of farmed fish are blamed for the spread of diseases and sea lice from caged to wild native stocks. The problem is exacerbated by farms being situated at the mouths of rivers where the returning wild salmon cannot avoid coming into close contact with them. There is also evidence of interbreeding between escaped farmed salmon and native wild salmon, with disease and escapees being suggested as reasons why native breeding stocks are declining. It has been suggested that this interference with the gene pool of native stocks is a threat to the survival of the wild Atlantic salmon. Another factor is the pollution generated by fish farms. The sea surrounding fish farms is a soup of uneaten food, fish faeces and nitrogenous products which can cause toxic algal blooms.

On the other hand salmon farming is worth around £500 million to the Scottish economy and provides livelihoods for thousands of people directly and even more in supporting sectors. Much of these jobs exist in rural areas where employment can be scarce. There is also demand for farmed salmon as a consumer product: it is a popular item in the shopping basket.

It is common for a debate like this to take the form of conservation versus development, where one side argues one thing and the other side argues something else. It need not be this way. Political parties and interest groups in capitalist countries have structured themselves around the concept of adversarial politics and so it is not surprising that the idea of conservation being one thing and development being another has written itself into the psyche of capitalist thinking.

It is often the case that capitalist economics values the wrong sorts of things. The gas leak in the Indian city of Bhopal that killed thousands of people provided growth to the economy because it created more employment in the clean-up. What is more valuable, jobs or clean air? Capitalist economics does not put a value on air or water, something essential to human survival. Yet the same economic system values people who get cancer or heart disease and are treated in hospital for it. Internationally renowned economist and Right Livelihood Award winner Professor Manfred Max-Neef has said that 'indiscriminate depletion of natural resources raises the GNP, as does a sick population which increases its consumption of pharmaceutical drugs and hospital services'. Or, as author and economist James Robertson has stated, 'It hardly makes sense, except to conventional economics, to suppose that the more a society has to spend in response to accidents, sickness and disease, the better off it must be.' What sort of system values things that are harmful to us but does not value things that are essential not only to our health and well-being but our very existence?

By focusing on the issue of fish farming through the lens of the economic system that created it we can see both what is wrong and right with the salmon farming industry. When talking of conservation and development it is not that one is 'bad' and the other 'good'. The fish farming industry is an example where economics came first and the environment was an after thought. This is not surprising because when salmon farming started in the 1970s there was a lot of enthusiasm to create jobs in rural Scotland. The wider environmental consequences were not known and it was only as the salmon farming industry developed that the environmental impacts became clear.

The lesson to be learned from fish farming is that when it comes to conservation and development a science-based approach to environmental sustainability is the bedrock on which development can take place – but before development begins. It is a system based around the precautionary principle which aims to protect both public health and the environment. The idea is that the burden of proof lies with the developer to demonstrate the value of any project.

A developer could argue that this was anti-capitalist and anti-competitive, but it is not. It is simply using economics to take *full* account of developments. Capitalist economics accounts for the production, distribution and consumption of goods and services. Yet that is only part of the life cycle of products. After the point of consumption much of the cycle remains unaccounted for. Developers and manufacturers of products and services are rarely held responsible for the depletion of resources and any pollution their activities cause. Instead governments and local authorities use taxpayers' money to pay for the disposal of waste through recycling schemes, landfill maintenance and incineration. They also have to pay for the monitoring and treatment of domestic and industrial pollution from the public purse. This means that it is the taxpayer and not the developer who pays for what happens after the point of consumption. Meantime consumer purchases are made in ignorance of true costs because there is an absence of any full life-cycle analysis.

A system of economics that includes a full life-cycle analysis of goods and services is a system that is not simply about wildlife protection but a system that looks at nature and people and how to protect livelihoods. Looking at things this way means that development is not necessarily anti-conservation, and conservation need not be seen as anti-development. Problems do arise when little account of social, environmental and economic impact is taken before developments proceed. When this happens a whole infrastructure of jobs and support services are created and become dependent on unsustainable resources. It is understandable therefore that environmentalists protest against certain developments, that developers argue when their plans are opposed, and that communities complain about potential job losses. All are victims of a system that takes little account of the depleting and polluting effects of production and distribution and does not account for what happens after the point of consumption (e.g. what to do with waste products).

Strange as it might seem, instead of fighting each other conservationists and developers might do well to work together to reorient the system. In the long term there is no real alternative because for humans to be healthy and prosperous the environment needs to be healthy and prosperous. The economy depends on the environment. To reverse the order is to play Russian roulette with our futures.

Leaning against the cage and peering in at these impersonations of their wild counterparts I sympathised with them. Some environmental philosophers would accuse me of anthropomorphism. They might ask how I could know that the creatures were suffering. Of course I realise the dangers of anthropomorphism and its tendency to over romanticise something.

However, these remain theoretical arguments. The philosophy I am talking about requires direct experience of its subject matter. Furthermore it is not just about experience but *verstehen*. The German sociologist Max Weber popularised this term, which describes an outside observer of a culture (e.g. an anthropologist) trying to interpret human behaviour from within the perspective of the culture itself, not as a distant, objective observer. I can apply this idea to my experience of the salmon.

Wild Atlantic salmon travel around two thousand miles from their feeding grounds in Greenland to arrive in Scotland. Once they get here they travel along the north coast or south down the east or west coasts in search of their river of birth and early development. In so doing they pass numerous rivers that are potentially 'false trails'. One of the marvels of nature and something still not fully understood is that after spending up to four years at sea the salmon's homing instinct is so strong that, with very few exceptions, each individual finds its way back to the river in which it was born.

Thinking of the listless creatures found in salmon cages I am reminded of the French sociologist Emile Durkheim's concept of *anomie*, a condition of society where changing rules leaves people not knowing what to expect from each other, eventually leading to a lack of consensus. I cannot speak of what these creatures really are experiencing but my guess is that it has something to do with confusion and normlessness. The same can be said of the big cats and bears in a zoo where the behavioural consequences of being caged can be observed. They wander aimlessly around their pens in a state of habitual displacement, unable to express their natural behaviour.

There was no more time for thinking about the Shadow Self, *verstehen* or *anomie* as a motorised RIB approached. The occupant told me that I was trespassing and asked me to paddle outside of the buoyed area. I had wondered if under the Scottish Outdoor Access Code I might have had a legal entitlement to be there and fleetingly contemplated an argument. But I suspected that this would be rather churlish and so I maintained my own counsel and headed out of the 'no canoeing zone' to look for a lunch spot.

Over lunch I saw a cormorant swim into view and begin diving for fish. I was reminded of how in different parts of the world cormorants have been used to catch fish for human consumption. Fishermen attach lines to the cormorants and put rings around their necks to prevent them from swallowing large fish. They are then released on their tethers and reined in when a fish is caught. In this way the cormorant can be used to harvest fish and the fishermen share the surplus catch.

It is far too simplistic to suggest that fish farming has something to learn from this method of fish harvesting. However, it is at least as simplistic to suggest that it has not. In addition to the 'precautionary principle' perhaps a 'scale principle' could be introduced to development. If development began first with small-scale activity and increased gradually then it could proceed with greater sensitivity towards the principles of environmental sustainability. Once again this is in line with Schumacher's thinking that *Small is Beautiful*. Exploring the extent to which the environment can support the economy is a challenge to the 'business as usual' approach of corporate industrial development.

There is no longer a natural water link between Loch Lochy and the River Lochy. During the construction of the Caledonian Canal the water level of Loch Lochy had to be raised, the river mouth relocated, and the river rerouted. It is now a physical impossibility to canoe from Loch Lochy into River Lochy. My map indicated two potential water outlets that I might be able to use to continue my journey. One is the Caledonian Canal, which I had already decided not to use. Another channel forms part of a hydro-electricity scheme. A line of buoys across its mouth prevent pleasure boat crews from accidentally mistaking it for the canal. There was a warning sign saying as much. It looked very calm and I could see from my map that after around six hundred metres it connects with the River Spean, which then runs into the River Lochy. I had seen before the confluence of this water channel with the Spean and knew that the water tumbles over a steep drop of sharp angular boulders held together by wire baskets. Apart from this obstacle I did not know what lay in between. I was tempted to paddle the stretch, thinking that when I got to the un-navigable confluence I would be able to portage around it. What I did not know was the timing of any water releases, meaning I could easily find myself starting off in calm water only to be caught up in a release that would send me hurtling down a steep-sided concrete channel with no means of escape. A stupid idea. I didn't need Shakespeare to convince me that discretion would be the better part of valour, and I decided to portage the final kilometre to the River Lochy.

Back on the water I looked forward to the remaining twelve kilometres downstream towards Fort William, the first time on the journey that I did not have to power against upstream currents. However, I hadn't accounted for the wind funnelled directly upstream. Despite my best paddling efforts I found myself being blown the wrong way into overhanging trees. In a fit of pique my Shadow Self revealed itself and I shouted, 'Let the bloody planet burn!' (or some unprintable version of that) to anybody close enough to listen.

I managed to travel downstream for around eight kilometres, using a combination of poling and paddling. After a day of mishaps and hard paddling into the wind I became eager to stop and eat. The roar of rapids in the distance convinced me that the excitement of negotiating them could wait for the next day, so

I settled into my camp routine in a beautiful oak wood slightly back and elevated from the river.

Another cold frosty morning dawned. Despite my lack of bodily fitness it was my wrists that hurt most. Pushing weakened wrists through the tight-fitting rubber cuffs of my dry top was painful, more so as it was cold. However, the pain was soon forgotten as the landscape unfolded. Ben Nevis, at one thousand, three hundred and forty-four metres the highest mountain in the United Kingdom, appeared with its flanks and peaks still covered in the last remnants of winter snow. Daydreaming under the ben's gaze and listening to the early morning dawn chorus, the sense of peace was overwhelming.

The promise of excitement at Torcastle rapid gradually replaced the peace as I prepared for my first downstream grade three rapid. The rapid narrowed to a V about six feet across, but in higher water the gap would probably widen to about twenty feet. I had paddled it before in higher water and my unladen canoe had taken on a lot of water.

Inspecting the rapid from the bank I decided to paddle and not portage. I managed to maintain my favoured line, avoiding a few partially submerged rocks on the approach, and I couldn't help smile with the sheer joy of it. A reprimand was needed though, as I had taken on a little water that needed to be bailed out.

The river flows south along a glaciated valley in a straight line to the sea. It suddenly turns left to form the rapid I had just descended, then right, then right again before turning left to its original southerly direction. On the map the water feature looks like a box shaped meander. It appears that the river has come up against a hard bedrock feature resistant to erosion and been deflected around it. It is this micro-topography that created the rocky waterfall. Between Loch Lochy and the sea it is the only rock sill throughout the length of the glaciated river channel. As the gorge opens up towards the end of the meander the river runs more gently and I could bask in its peace, sheltered from the wind by rocky banks.

6

Paradigms lost and found

THE WIND HAD DIED DOWN IN THE MORNING AND WITH THE sun up it felt right to slow down and look around. In a pool of still water I watched the newly arrived sand martins. They are unusual birds in that they do not build a nest. Their scientific name gives a clue about their lifestyle – *Riparia riparia*, with 'riparia' referring to riverbanks. Instead of a nest they excavate holes in the side of banks such as those that line the River Lochy. Like the Atlantic salmon they are migratory; wintering in Africa they arrive in Scotland in March. They were busy as I watched them, lining their burrows with feathers and plant materials in anticipation of breeding.

Further downstream the standing ruins of Inverlochy Castle appear as a reminder of some of the countless clan feuds that took place throughout Scottish history. Here in 1431 the MacDonalds defeated the Stewarts, then in 1645 there was a particularly nasty event that marks out Scotland's involvement in what became known as the Wars of the Three Kingdoms (Scotland, England

and Ireland). The war was not just between nations – Scotland was at war with itself. On one side stood the Royalists, loyal to the English King, Charles I, who advocated the divine right of the monarchy. They were led by the Marquess of Montrose who spearheaded a number of campaigns in the king's name.

On the other side were the Covenanters who deeply resented Charles' interference in the affairs of the Presbyterian Church of Scotland. It was against their religion for anyone other than God to be the spiritual leader of the church; hence their antipathy towards a monarch appropriating that role. The Marquess of Argyll, Chief of the Clan Campbell, rallied his troops in defence of the faith. Those who had Covenanting sympathies were persecuted and the practice of Presbyterianism came to be classed as a treasonable offence; church ministers could be summarily executed. When these two forces met they were fuelled by a powerful combination of differing religious and cultural beliefs and generations of clan feuding. Montrose won the battle and there followed a massacre of up to one thousand five hundred of the vanquished Campbells.

The peaceful landscape belies its murderous history, but in the background Ben Nevis gazes down on the spot just as it did when those events unfolded more than three hundred years ago. Under the ben's dominating presence I was filled with a great sense of sorrow for all those who died at the castle, as well as others who continue to die in conflicts around the world. I needed to find an outlet for the melancholy trapped inside me and began to sing a song about a later war. It starts:

Well, how do you do, Private William McBride,
Do you mind if I sit here down by your graveside?
And rest for awhile in the warm summer sun

I've been walking all day, and I'm nearly done
And I see by your gravestone you were only nineteen
When you joined the glorious fallen in nineteen-sixteen
Well, I hope you died quick and I hope you died clean
Or, Willie McBride, was it slow and obscene?

As the final words were carried away from my lips by the light breeze to spread over the scene of beauty and battle, I thanked the Scottish singer-songwriter Eric Bogle for putting to words and song the horrors and futility of war.

There are good reasons for quoting an anti-war song in a book about the relationship between people and nature. The most obvious is the social and environmental destruction inherent in armed conflict. The Kuwaiti oil fires are one example in recent memory, when Iraqi military forces in retreat adopted a 'scorched earth' policy to prevent economically valuable oil fields from falling into the hands of their enemies. The fires burned for several months, polluting the atmosphere, while unburned oil pooled in large lakes, threatening to pollute groundwater reservoirs. Another example is the atomic bombings of the Japanese cities of Hiroshima and Nagasaki, which killed over two hundred thousand people, either instantly or within weeks of the blasts, and unknown thousands died afterwards as a consequence of radiation exposure, burns and lack of medical attention. The radiation too would have affected drinking water supplies and agricultural production. The environmental impacts of war are endless. What is clear, though, is that when you trace the impacts of war through the hunter-gatherer, agriculturalist and industrialist epochs, the means by which humans can kill and maim each other has grown dramatically in scope and scale.

Just as the military refer to the accidental killing of civilians as 'collateral damage' so too does the environment become incidental. The very life support systems that we depend on for our health and well-being are relegated to some subordinate status as the causes and freedoms of various nation states and interest groups are fought out on a regular basis.

It may appear overly romantic and politically naïve to rely on the lyrics of a folk song as an alternative to mainstream politics. This is not the point. The point is that Eric Bogle is a 'man of conscience' demonstrating his 'capacity for moral awareness' – Adam Smith's words again. Here is a folk singer raging against the system. His repertoire of songs is full of political commentary, the causes of environmental destruction and criticisms of the greed that fuels capitalism. Systems change when enough people rage at them and the electorate do not have to rely on the actions of politicians as the only way of bringing about change.

The problem is that in war each side always think they are right and their cause just, and that the other side are wrong and their cause unjust. When the MacDonalds fought the Stewarts in 1431, and the Marquess of Montrose fought the Marquess of Argyll in 1645, and in every battle ever fought before and since, all sides thought they were in the right. These beliefs were sufficiently strong that leaders could mobilise their followers to fight. Can they both be right at the same time? Can one be more right than the other, or can they both be wrong?

I have some personal experience of these questions, which I began asking when I joined the British Army at the age of fifteen. Well, the questions did not begin then, but my experiences of the army provided the basis from which they would later arise. Not long after I joined, my regiment was sent on active service.

At the time it seemed like my duty and I had no qualms about what might lie ahead. I had trained to go and fight for Queen and country; it seemed so obvious. Underneath this apparent noble gesture there lurked something more sinister. I wondered what it might be like to kill somebody.

A lack of worldly experience, a general lack of critical thinking skills together with effective military conditioning proved to be a powerful combination that determined the way I thought. Reflecting on it now, it seems almost inevitable that I would end up thinking that the world was made up of good people and bad people. Armed with this simplistic vision of the world and its people was what made me think about killing. When you come to believe that the people you fight alongside are self-evidently good (and why not, they are your friends and extended family) it is very easy not to ever think about what the cause is. When this premise is formed as fact in your mind it is not such a large leap to the conclusion that those you fight against are bad. This train of thought can easily lead to the next conclusion – that the bad should be punished for their misdeeds – and hence the logical justification for killing and war is in place.

It would be easy for senior military personnel, and indeed others not exposed to the military, to trivialise the simplicity of this argument. However, for me at that time it was as simple as that. It would be another ten years or so, when I went to university, before I began to see the shades of grey between the black and white.

To be clear, this is not a critique of the military. While I am disinclined to think of warfare as the best means of conflict resolution, I would not be at the front of any pacifist queue that argued for a demilitarised world. I am pretty sure that any attempts towards world pacifism would only offer opportunities for some interest group or nation state eager to militarise and take advantage of the situation. No, this is not about the military and warfare. It is more about how people come to think of what is right and what is wrong.

I am now not proud that I once wanted to kill people. Nowadays I am vehemently opposed to the taking of human life, by whatever method. However, this powerful contrast between then and now has been a formative experience in my life. It reminds me how the experiences we have, as well as the people around us, are important to the way our values are negotiated, formed, maintained and changed. I understand therefore why the MacDonalds and the Stewarts, the Covenanters and the Royalists, fought over their grievances and freedoms. The leaders may well have been able to articulate what these freedoms and grievances were, but I am more interested in why the followers followed. The followers did not instigate the wars, but nevertheless chose to go with their leaders. What was it that led some people to follow leaders, and for both leaders and followers to follow causes? Were they all just simply victims of certain circumstances? Were they motivated by revenge following previous battles involving their families and ancestors? It is the Shadow Self that asks these questions.

I launched my canoe and followed the escape route of the fleeing Campbells down-river towards the sea. Fresh water meets salt water at Loch Linnhe, marking my first crossing of Scotland on the trip. The town of Fort William came into view and I landed at the foot of the seventeenth century ruins known as the Old Fort. An interpretive board explained how Fort William got its name. Its Gaelic name is *An Gearasdan*, meaning 'The Garrison', hence Fort; and the town was named after the king, hence William.

I was drawn naturally to explore the ruins until the cold wind blowing through the holes in my clothes reminded me that I had landed for another reason.

I made for the nearest outdoor equipment retailer with a shopping list to buy glue and replace the old trousers, waterproof over-trousers and sandals, none of which now had any redeeming features. Crossing the threshold was like entering Aladdin's Cave – it is no wonder that consumer culture is so successful. This shop was full of things that I did not need but on every shelf there was a huge range of items all shouting in a loud voice 'buy me', 'buy me'. The whole process is so seductive but my Shadow Self shouts at least as loud. I checked clothing to identify the country of origin so I could make a choice based on carbon emissions. The closer the place of production to the point of purchase the less transport pollution that purchase causes, but the labels do not give any other information that might help me to make choices based on conscience. I would like some help with the relative merits of buying synthetic versus natural materials. It is not beyond the means of the retail industry to provide this information and it would be most welcome.

The real problem is not so much what is on sale, whether 'environmentally friendly' or not, the problem remains that of self-interest. It is all too easy to look at an attractive item in a shop and find some tenuous reason to justify buying it. I am not trying to suggest an ideal world, some utopia in which consumers can buy 'environmentally friendly' goods free of guilt or burden. It seems pointless to envision what a sustainable world might look like without giving thought to what this means for everyday people going about their everyday lives. People need starting points as well as visions. If the gap between the vision and people's everyday lives is too great then no-one knows where to start. This only leads to some combination of helplessness, disempowerment or even denial that there is a planetary emergency.

My own way of dealing with my purchases was to buy only what I needed at that time. Need in this sense was defined by function (without these clothes I would literally freeze), quality (I wanted the clothes to stand up to the rigours of the trip), necessity (I had no other clothes to wear), and alternatives (the charity shops I visited first did not have suitable second-hand alternatives). These ideas of need could be developed further but the point here is that the act of consumption can be, and perhaps ought to be, based on principles. Without stated principles wants are confused with needs and the system of rampant capitalism prevails as consumers plunder the planet.

It is important to note that I am not singling out outdoor shops for criticism. I am using this as an example of something much larger and systemic in the retail world, which includes all sorts of clothing and equipment retail as well as the markets for holidays, food and drink, electronic equipment and cars. However, the scope of the problem seems so great it leaves individuals asking where they can start. With one foot in the present to guide our everyday short-term actions, and one foot in the future to guide our aspirations towards the values and principles of sustainability, there may just be a position from which we can find creative impulses to make changes. This is the difference between the rampant consumer (who confuses wants with needs) and the conscious consumer (who modifies their purchases on the basis of knowledge and moderation).

When I was back on the water and resplendent in my new

clothing the gentle waves lapped playfully around my canoe. They were not large enough to come pouring over the gunnel. Looking over my left shoulder I could see the mass of Ben Nevis begin to recede into the distance but, looking ahead, I noticed a yacht under sail some eight hundred metres away coming towards me at speed. My canoe is green and its profile in the water low compared to those standing up in the yacht, so it was a good policy to assume that I had not been seen. In terms of thinking through avoidance strategies it is advisable to act on the principle that 'Might is Right'. I had already been feeling rather insignificant thinking about war and my temporary existence, but in that moment as the boat bore down I was reminded of how important to me that feeble existence was.

I could see two sailors; one was dropping and gathering the sails and the other was pulling furiously on the cord of an outboard motor that did not appear to be starting. Furthermore, nobody seemed to be steering. The boat closed to about two hundred metres and the outboard showed no sign of starting. The distance between us became alarmingly close and I had to take action to avoid a collision, so I turned towards the shore, aiming for shallow water, where my tormentor would run aground before hitting me. At one hundred metres and closing I turned my canoe at right angles and paddled furiously. I was very exposed for two reasons. Firstly, I had to make headway into the wind to get out of the boat's path; secondly, being broadside I presented a much larger target. A collision seemed inevitable until the person trying to start the outboard motor threw an anchor out the back. At first it seemed to make no impression but then the yacht slowed up and stopped. Either their charts said they were over sand, and they knew it, or they got a lucky break. Had the anchor snagged on a rock I guess they'd have had a spot of bother as the anchor held fast and they were thrown off balance.

The sailor at the back was wearing spectacles and I wondered if he had just put them on. The yacht was a Suffolk Beach Punt with gaff yawl rig. In their efforts to stop the Punt neither of the sailors had noticed my presence. As I paddled past I hailed them and enquired after their technical problems, thinking that the events of the last few minutes must have been fairly stressful for them too. With stiff upper lips they assured me that all was in order and they were in complete control. Relieved that the atoms of my body were going to remain part of me for a little longer I could not resist a parting shot. Resorting to humour based on stereotypes I enquired how the gin stocks were holding out. Not waiting for an answer I made a rather slow escape into the strong headwind.

No sooner had I made my escape than the bolt that held my seat in place sheared and I fell to the bottom of the canoe. One of the advantages of a canoe is that it has two seats, so I could just turn the canoe round and with some trim adjustment continue paddling. I had to be content with this temporary measure because ahead lay the Corran Narrows. The tidal stream had already started and if I delayed too long the flow would be too strong for me to canoe against.

The movement of the tides results from the gravitational effects of the sun and the moon. Here on the west coast of Scotland the tide comes from the south and, like a slow-moving river, works its way north. The tide will run slowly like this for around six hours, creeping up the beaches it passes along the way. After a short period of slack water the tide will then ebb to the south for six hours, draining the beaches it so recently filled. This ebb and flow continues unabated until it meets a constriction like the Corran Narrows, through which it must pass to fill Loch Linnhe and, beyond that, Loch Eil. Together these sea lochs are nearly thirty kilometres long and between one and two kilometres wide. A vast amount of water pours in and out of the sea lochs as it meets this constriction, which is only three hundred metres wide, and as it is squeezed through the gap the water accelerates.

At its fastest the tidal race will run at a speed of five knots, it creates a force impossible for me to progress against. However, the race does not run at five knots for the whole six hours. It speeds up gradually to five knots over three hours and slows down again over the next three hours. Within the first hour of the flow it only runs at a fraction of its total speed, so it was likely that I could make some progress against it.

By the time I approached the narrows the water was rushing towards me like a river. The tidal stream was already in its second hour. To continue I needed to paddle upstream for two hundred metres to a point on the opposite side where the constriction widens and the current eases. There was an added complication in that a car ferry constantly moved back and forth across the current behind me. With one last look to make sure that the ferry was on the slipway loading cars I set off into the flow.

Within thirty seconds it was clear that I was not going anywhere. I was stuck in the middle of the current not going forwards and not going back. I had prepared myself for this eventuality and decided in advance that if it happened I would continue to the other side where I might just be able to line the canoe along the side of the opposite bank. The problem was that the ferry had started to move and I was only one hundred metres upstream of it and beginning to lose a little momentum against the strengthening current. Despite my best efforts I was drifting slowly but surely back towards the ferry. I could not afford to turn too much otherwise the current would push me sideways into its path. With the ferry's engine roaring right behind me, it was the second time that day my heart was in my mouth. I held my nerve and turned the angle ever so slightly towards the bank, kept the power on, and with huge relief reached the slack water eddy on the left bank. In this position of safety I could see the ferry passengers watching me. I guess they saw a fairly polished performance, but I did think that there must be easier ways of saving the planet!

I had a go at lining the canoe up the left bank but a combination of the strengthening current and difficult underfoot conditions convinced me that this wasn't going to work either. I considered portaging over the rocks, heather and hummocks, but I was not in the mood for such energetic exercise. Instead I settled down on an outcrop by the side of the tidal stream to wait until it was ready to allow me passage.

One way to think about whether something is right or wrong is to step back from the issue itself and view it through a cultural lens. If you asked someone if murder was right or wrong they would most likely say wrong. No doubt some people would say that it depends, but the fact remains that we have a legal system that forbids it. The biblical enunciation 'Thou Shall Not Kill' remains a powerful cultural legacy, and there is a general belief within societies around the world that an individual has a right to go about their own life without it being taken by another person.

In *The web of life* Fritjof Capra calls this cultural lens a paradigm, which he defines as 'a constellation of concepts, values, perceptions, and practices shared by a community, which forms a particular vision of reality that is the basis of the way the community organises itself.' The constellation of shared values Capra refers to is the glue that holds a culture together. It's not that the constellation is so fixed that ideas cannot be debated or laws changed, more that paradigms act as a blueprint on which roles are understood, and so form a base over which any change must be negotiated. It is not necessary for everyone to agree about all things for a paradigm to exist, but there must be sufficient agreement about most things for the culture to survive. By looking at an issue through a cultural lens you consider the values and beliefs of the culture itself in order to understand why some things are defined as 'right' and others as 'wrong'.

A paradigm therefore is a living tradition that helps us to act out our daily lives in accordance with our values. Because it is a living tradition it goes to the very heart of our individual being, our role within a community and how we conduct ourselves in that community. Paradigms provide the possibility for powerful allegiances to develop within communities.

Something else about paradigms is that they can be so pervasive that the values that people act upon are often invisible on a daily basis. For instance, why is it considered rude to spit? Why do you not want to be seen picking your nose in public? Why do men wear ties? There are reasons, but these are not part of our everyday experiences, whereas the actions are. The actions of individuals and communities are formed around assumptions and values that are often unconscious, unspoken or even forgotten.

It is possible, therefore, for people within communities to go about their lives unaware of the values their community possesses. This is the case when individuals act on the basis of repeated behaviour – a 'this is the way we have always done it' attitude. In this way the values remain invisible even though the practice continues. While there is nothing inherently wrong with people acting out their lives on the basis of unacknowledged assumptions, there is a shadow side. For me it explains why as a seventeen year old soldier I was so keen to kill someone without thinking it was important and without understanding my motivations for doing so. It also explains to some extent the reasons why the clans followed their chiefs into battle at Inverlochy Castle. These men were prepared to make the ultimate sacrifice on the basis of unacknowledged assumptions – so strong that they were prepared to die for them, yet so invisible that they may not even have known those assumptions existed.

The way we think about our values and what is important to us is central to more fully understanding the relationship between people and nature. If unacknowledged assumptions are the basis on which we often act, then what do these assumptions look like when they are made visible? The questions just keep coming.

The flood tide had reached its zenith and begun to slow down. I waited until it dropped off sufficiently before trying again. The current remained powerful but close to the rocks there were a number of counter eddies which flowed upstream. By linking these I was left finally with one last rocky outcrop to pass, around which the current was still quite strong. To negotiate it successfully I needed to move back down the eddy and then accelerate up it, cross the eddy at speed and at a very slight angle into the current and paddle hard for about twenty metres where the constriction finally opened out and the flow eased.

The Corran Narrows separates Upper Loch Linnhe from

Lower Loch Linnhe, which opens into a wide bay and then continues south-westward to meet the Atlantic Ocean. Hugging the coast to the east would take me further inland by way of Loch Leven. When I was planning the journey I was concerned about the following six kilometres of coastline because of its exposure to the prevailing south-westerly winds. If they proved to be strong then the most difficult part of the stretch would be the exposed headland called Rubha Cuil-cheanna which points directly south-west. My canoe was not designed for the sea. Although it coped well on the large inland lochs the sea's swell is much larger. Thankfully the wind was light and with darkness approaching I tried to get round the headland. The forecast for the day after was for the wind to pick up and I didn't want to be stranded on the wrong side of the headland with the sheltered waters of Loch Leven so close.

As I came nearer the headland small rocky cliffs appeared. Waves crashed up against them and bounced back. On their return they met the next set of waves coming in, creating a phenomenon known as clapotis. Clapotis can be dangerous in strong winds, when the waves become higher because of the strength of their collisions. The sea also becomes more confused because the smooth and rounded waves transform into something jagged, irregular and steep. It can be so turbulent that you sometimes have to canoe as much as a kilometre out to sea to avoid its worst effects.

However, on this occasion the clapotis is playful, exciting even given my rather precarious position. When the bolt on my seat sheared earlier I had turned the canoe round and used the other seat to sit on. Although the hull is symmetrical the seats are positioned asymmetrically. When paddling double the back seat is positioned slightly nearer to the stern than the front seat is to the bow and this allows room for the front person's legs. However, when solo paddling it is common for the paddler to turn the canoe around and paddle it 'back to front'. Using the front seat with the canoe 'the wrong way round' brings the solo paddler's weight nearer the centre of the canoe and helps with the fore and aft trim.

This is what I was doing when my seat broke. Because I turned it round I had to sit in the seat I would have been in if someone else were in the front. The problem is that sitting very near the back of the canoe is the point where it is at its narrowest. With no-one in the front to stabilise the canoe my lateral stability was compromised by the constant search for a finely tuned balance point. Happily in those conditions it was not a problem; I could easily slip off the seat and move forward onto my knees, adopting a more stable position. It was pleasant to let the waves roll under the finely balanced craft and tempt the clapotis to capsize me.

The sense of playfulness turned to awe as I rounded the headland and Glencoe came into view. The glen is famous for its own clan feuding; in 1692 two companies of soldiers led by Captain Robert Campbell, loyal to King William of Orange, murdered the local population of MacDonalds because of their Jacobite sympathies. The Glencoe massacre has its own place in the social history of Scotland but at that moment it was the natural history that held my attention. I had already thought enough about the consequences and futility of war and found catharsis in the beauty of the scenery.

The glen is dominated by one of the most easily identifiable mountain landmarks in Scotland. The Pap of Glencoe sits at the western edge of the famous Aonach Eagach ridge. Its distinctive conical shape looks like the horn of a rhinoceros, with the nearby flank of Sgorr nam Fiannaidh forming its forehead. I have yet to scramble along its airy ridge, and perhaps that was why its proximity was particularly alluring.

Nearing the end of a long exciting day, and in fading light, I realised that there were no ideal camp spots nearby. Finding a campsite in the dark is never easy. Once before I had landed my sea kayak in pitch darkness and searched around a rocky shore for a suitable spot. Stumbling over the uneven ground I ended up standing on the rotting carcass of a seal and my foot disappeared up to the shin in its putrefying flesh. It's tricky sharing a tent with someone after such an experience and I resolved then always to camp before dark.

I managed to find an old, disused boatshed full of beer cans, whisky bottles and broken glass, which looked a possibility. With no prospect of a better camp spot and remembering the smelly seal incident my mind was made up. I looked out the holed trousers I had so recently replaced in Fort William; they made a good rag to clear away the worst of the debris. With a roof over my head there was no need to put the tent up. My temporary dry home also provided me with an opportunity to re-glue the broken mast step.

With all my chores done, the crossing of Scotland merited some celebration and I resolved to find out if the hotel marked on my map had a pub. When I found it I counted my blessings that I had stopped to buy new trousers in Fort William: there was no way I would have worn my holed trousers in public. It had been embarrassing enough wearing them to the shop to replace them. It seems that there may be limits to an anti-consumerist approach to life. Sporting my brand new trousers and feeling like a ragged-trousered fashion icon I walked confidently into the bar and ordered a pint.

Map 3 – The Atlantic to the North Sea

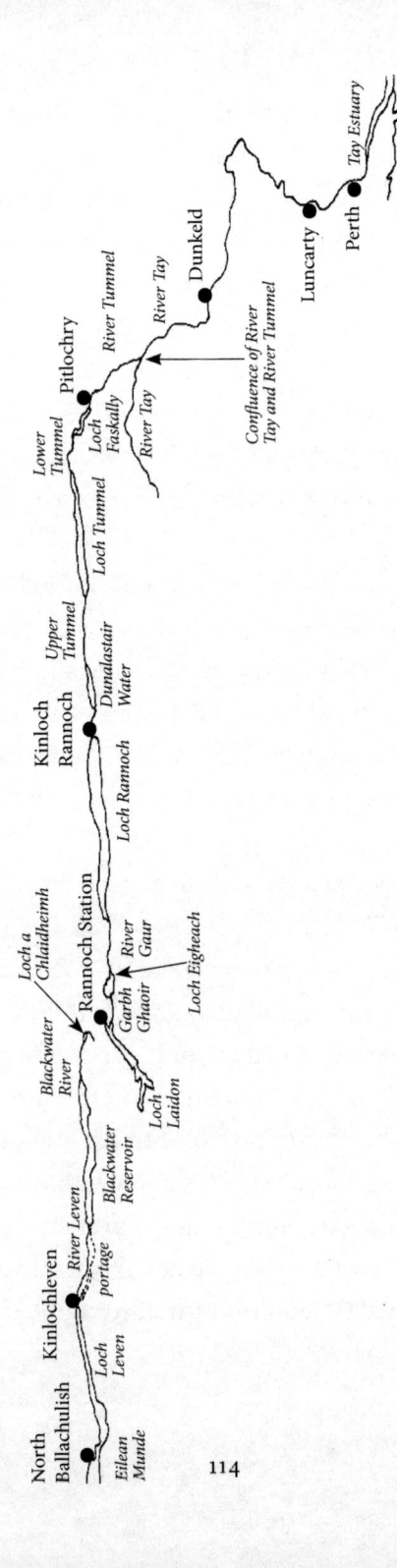

7

The changing climate

Looking out from my first roof-covered sleep for a week I could see that the sea was flat calm. The view on its own was worth *Canoeing around the Cairngorms*. The guilliemots (*Uria aalge*) provided a welcome sight; they were the first I had seen for more than a year, reminding me once again what the inland dweller misses when too long away from the sea. The name *Uria* is from the Greek, meaning 'to dive', and it is not long before they live up to their name by disappearing under the surface, the only sign they were ever there being the expanding rings of concentric circles on the water.

I was eager to be on my way and not having to pack the tent speeded things up. Just ahead there was another constriction between Loch Linnhe and Loch Leven at Ballachulish, where once again the tide runs at five knots. There are also overfalls, created where the sea is relatively shallow. Just like a horizontal constriction such as the Corran Narrows, the shallow seabed creates a vertical constriction. Here at Ballachulish the sea gets quite lumpy as it is forced through the gap.

I didn't need tide tables, navigational charts or other tidal information for the Ballachulish stretch as I could work out what I needed to know from my own observations and predictions. The night before I watched the tide rise until 1830 which meant that roughly twelve and a half hours later, at 0700, it would be high again. By leaving the boatshed at 0530 I could get to the narrows at the period between the tide coming in and starting to go out again. The slack tide lasts around half an hour and would allow for a straightforward passage through the narrows. Although my calculations were very rough and made no allowance for any local tidal variations, they were good enough to see me pass under the road bridge and into the shelter of Loch Leven as predicted.

There are several islands at the mouth of Loch Leven and I had planned to land on one, not least because I had missed breakfast. The first island is Eilean Choinneich, on which lots of herring gulls (*Larus argentatus*) were paired off, looking like they had claimed the entire island as a breeding colony. Keen not to disturb them I resolved to come back another time when it was not the nesting season. There was also some degree of self-interest in moving on because the gulls are large and their incessant squawks loud. I was not ready to share my dining area with such noisy neighbours.

The next island is called Eilean Munde after St. Mundus, one of St. Columba's disciples. I had hoped to land there when planning the journey. The island is the traditional cemetery for the people of Glencoe and the burial place for the MacDonalds from the 1692 massacre. However, a melancholic hangover remained from the visit to Inverlochy Castle and I resolved to find somewhere less gloomy to eat.

In the last chapter I explained why I am preoccupied with values and why they are important in understanding the relationship between people and nature. During my studies, I learned from Barry, Pete and Nev about global ecological problems such as climate change, species extinction, desertification, the growing of genetically modified crops, radioactive leaks from nuclear reprocessing plants and the 'hole' in the ozone layer. The fact that a growing human population could have such an effect on the environment made a large enough impression on me that I knew it would become my life's work. However serious these issues were at the time, I had little idea how quickly thereafter their gravity would increase, and how the rate of change would increase.

Carbon spirals around the planet as it is exchanged between its four major reservoirs: atmosphere, biosphere, hydrosphere and lithosphere. The carbon cycle involves fossil fuels such as coal, oil and natural gas. During the Carboniferous period (between two hundred and ninety and three hundred and fifty-five million years ago) vegetation that died and decayed was buried and eventually through the actions of pressure and heat formed coal. When marine organism sediments settle on the seabed some find their way into porous rock where they decay and form oil and natural gas. In these ways large deposits of carbon were locked up in the lithosphere.

Much of the energy from the Sun that is stored in vegetation remains stored when the vegetation transforms into coal. Because coal is readily combustible it releases energy easily, and this is one of the key reasons it was and remains such a valuable commodity. Coal was the source of energy that fuelled the steam engine, which in turn powered the factories that spawned the Industrial Revolution. However, one of the effects of burning coal is that it releases carbon into the atmosphere in the form of carbon dioxide. As the Industrial Revolution expanded, the world's economies grew and there was a greater demand for goods, and the market responded by making more commodities. In this way a carbon-dependent economy grew larger and larger. To meet consumer demand more factories were built, more coal was burned and factory chimneys released more carbon dioxide into the atmosphere. The freedoms, luxuries and necessities that generations of people living in the industrialist epoch have enjoyed are all the products of a carbon-fuelled economy.

Until the industrialist epoch the flow of carbon in circulation was fairly regular and stable. All this changed with the Industrial Revolution and its dependence on coal as a source of energy. The burning of fossil fuels has transferred unprecedented amounts of carbon from the lithosphere into the atmosphere. George Monbiot, a leading international commentator on climate change, says that 'carbon dioxide (CO_2) levels have been rising over the past century, faster than at any time over the past 20,000 years'.

In *An inconvenient truth*, Al Gore looks at the implications of the increasing amounts of carbon dioxide in the atmosphere.

> The Sun's energy enters the atmosphere in the form of light waves and heats up the Earth. Some of that energy warms the Earth and then is re-radiated back into space in the form of infrared waves. Under normal conditions, a portion of the outgoing infrared radiation is naturally trapped by the atmosphere – and that is a good thing, because it keeps the temperature on Earth within comfortable bounds…The problem we now face is that this thin layer of atmosphere is being thickened by huge quantities of human-caused carbon dioxide … and as

it thickens it traps a lot of the infrared radiation that would otherwise escape the atmosphere and continue out to the universe. As a result, the temperature of the Earth's atmosphere – and oceans – is getting dangerously warmer.

Gore is describing what is often referred to as the 'greenhouse effect'. Carbon dioxide is one of the major so-called greenhouse gases, along with methane, nitrous oxide and fluorocarbons. All these are natural components of the atmosphere and essential in regulating the temperature of the Earth to an average of 59°F (15°C). Without them the temperature would be about 0°F (−18°C).

Climate scientists are now concerned with what happens when these naturally occurring gases in the atmosphere are increased as a result of human activity. The Intergovernmental Panel on Climate Change (IPCC) draws on the work of leading climate scientists throughout the world and to date has published five Assessment Reports. These represent the most comprehensive assemblage of scientific data on climate change ever written. Their authors, leading climate scientists from around the world, include some Nobel Laureates.

The IPCC's 2014 *Summary for Policy Makers* stated that 'human influence on the climate system is clear, and recent anthropogenic emissions of greenhouse gases are the highest in history. Recent climate changes have had widespread impacts on human and natural systems'. Furthermore, there is evidence that precipitation has increased significantly in parts of North and South America, central Asia and Northern Europe. There is also evidence that in some areas of the world heat waves and intense tropical cyclone activity are more frequent, as well as evidence of plants migrating poleward and upward in response to temperature changes and earlier springs. In marine ecosystems algal, plankton and fish stocks are being affected by changes such as salinity concentrations.

The IPCC concludes that change to the climate system is unequivocal, and that many of the changes observed are unprecedented. The atmosphere and ocean have warmed, amounts of snow and ice have diminished, and the sea level has risen.

So here are the world's experts on climate change saying that the evidence is unequivocal that the climate is warming. Yet there are a minority who doubt. George Monbiot points out that the doubt is fuelled by what he calls 'the denial industry'. Chief among these is the fossil fuel industry, which boasts some of the most profitable corporations in the world. They are responsible for funding research units, community groups and other organisations that in turn claim there is no scientific consensus over climate change. As worldwide leaders of the oil and gas industry and major benefactors of the wealth that fossil fuels create this is to be expected given their vested interests. The confusion is maintained by some quarters of the media which, in keeping with adversarial norms, pit climate change experts against climate change deniers, thereby maintaining in the public eye a view that the science is not clear. It is easy therefore for the public to believe that consensus does not exist.

It remains important, though, that the climate change deniers have their say. Doubt can generate more criticality in terms of scientific enquiry and where it does, more clarity may well ensue. Also, contrary views are to be welcomed in any country that values free speech. However, it is important to establish the difference between evidence and rhetoric. The rhetoric of the climate change deniers is based on limited evidence which is consistently refuted by the evidence provided by the IPCC. This point is most important because there is a danger that the general public will become confused by experts who argue that climate change is real and present and others who deny it. Faced with conflicting evidence it is easy for ordinary folk to conclude that if the experts can't sort it out then neither can they.

It is easy for the sceptics to associate these ideas with over-reacting environmentalists. However, any notion that climate change is the fanciful notion of a few 'left-wing greens' was finally dismissed with the publication in the UK of the Stern Review (2006), and Stern, as noted earlier, is no mad environmentalist.

The Stern Review is a seven-hundred-page report commissioned by the UK government to establish the effects of climate change on the world economy. The report states:

> The stocks of greenhouse gases in the atmosphere (including carbon dioxide, methane, nitrous oxides and a number of gases that are from industrial processes) are rising, as a result of human activity ... The current level or stock of greenhouse gases in the atmosphere is equivalent to around 430 parts per million (ppm) CO_2, compared with only 280ppm before the Industrial Revolution.

In terms of economic solutions, the Stern Review estimates that it would take an investment of one per cent of global GDP to avoid the worst effects of climate change, if that investment were immediate. However, failure to invest now could mean a loss of twenty per cent to the world economy. In simple terms, if the global economy acts now it will save itself money in the long term. It must be inspiring to the captains of industry to learn that there are still market mechanisms available to them despite the harmful effects of growth economics.

So here is a mainstream economist recognising that climate change is real and present and, like the IPCC, the Stern Review attributes the increase of greenhouse gases in the atmosphere to anthropogenic causes. This consensus is continually growing. Professor David King, previously the UK's chief scientist, said that 'climate change is a far greater threat to the world than international terrorism'.

This statement was made in 2004 and is remarkable not least for its timing in relation to other world affairs. The September 11 attacks on the World Trade Centre occurred in 2001. In response and, in the same year, the United States and United Kingdom launched a military offensive in Afghanistan. In 2003 the same countries formed a coalition and invaded Iraq. So in 2004 the so-called 'War on Terror' was at its height, giving an indication of how serious David King viewed the threat of climate change.

Measurements indicate that the Arctic is currently warming at twice the global rate. As a result, as Mark Lynas writes in *Six Degrees*, 'across the entire Arctic, glaciers and ice caps have lost 400 cubic kilometres of volume over the past forty years.' Currently, with less than one degree of global warming, mountain glaciers too are already melting. Mount Kiliminjaro's eleven-thousand-year-old ice field measured just over twelve square kilometres in 1912, and was reduced to just over two square kilometres in 2000. While it is recognised that deforestation has partly contributed to the loss of Kiliminjaro's ice the same cannot be said of Greenland. The IPCC reports that 'current models suggest virtually complete elimination of the Greenland icesheet and a resulting contribution to sea level rise of about seven metres if global average warming were sustained for millennia in excess of 1.9 to 4.6°C relative to pre-industrial values.'

In recent years, reduced precipitation has created a drought in the Amazon, leaving exposed riverbanks dried and weathered. Erosion, sandstorms and forest fires have transformed the landscape, threatening the lives and livelihoods of local inhabitants. The Amazonian ecosystem may recover from these hot, dry spells, so long as deforestation is halted and the temperature remains less than one degree warmer than now.

But although the implication for the Amazon is that it is not yet too late, a less than one degree rise in average global temperatures has already proved too much for islands in the Pacific. Islands such as Tuvalu already experience regular flooding events as sea levels rise. Even if greenhouse gas emissions stopped increasing tomorrow, Lynas argues, it would still be too late to prevent the migration of the human inhabitants, leaving behind a landscape rendered infertile by salinity and slowly succumbing to the rising tide – eventually to be submerged.

What is most significant is that these changes have occurred as a result of a global temperature increase of less than one degree. Bear in mind that estimates warn of a possible six degree rise over the next one hundred years. George Monbiot provides an even starker assessment of the situation if the temperature were to rise by two degrees:

> If in the year 2030, carbon dioxide concentrations in the atmosphere remain as high as they do today, the likely result is two degrees centigrade of warming (above pre-industrial levels). Two degrees is the point beyond which major ecosystems begin collapsing. Having, until then, absorbed carbon dioxide, they begin to release it.

Beyond this point, in other words, climate change is out of our hands: it will accelerate without our help

Going towards the higher end of the scale Lynas states:

> With five degrees of global warming, an entirely new planet is coming into being – one largely unrecognisable from the Earth we know today. The remaining ice sheets are eventually eliminated from both poles. Rainforests have already burned up and disappeared. Rising sea levels have inundated coastal cities and are beginning to penetrate far inland into continental interiors. Humans are herded into shrinking zones of habitability by the twin crises of drought and flood. Inland areas see temperatures ten or more degrees higher than now.

Lynas refers to the degree-by-degree increase as Dante's Inferno where Dante is led through the corridors of hell.

The science of climate change is fascinating but I do not want to dwell on it and fill these pages with information that is readily available and more comprehensive than I can relay. The IPCC reports and the Stern Review are available on the worldwide web and there is an abundance of scientific papers, journals and popular science books that deal with the technical information. The inclusion of this snapshot of climate change here is firstly to acknowledge the severity of its consequences, but more importantly to pose the question 'so what?' The time to debate the existence of climate change and whether its causes are anthropogenic is now past.

However, the knowledge provided by science and the

understanding of the consequences of climate change are useless unless acted upon, and there remains a gap between knowledge and action. George Monbiot suggests that the reason for this is

> the connection between cause and effect seems so improbable. By turning on the lights, filling the kettle, taking the children to school, driving to the shops, we are condemning other people to death. We never chose to do this. We do not see ourselves as killers. We perform these acts without passion or intent.

Monbiot reminds us that poorer nations such as drought-ridden Ethiopia emit as little as one four-hundredth of the carbon dioxide that richer nations such as Luxembourg do. He also refers to Bangladesh, which regularly experiences major flooding events. Countries like Ethiopia and Bangladesh, already experiencing the more obvious effects of warming, are like canaries in a coal mine, if richer nations choose to pay heed. Richer nations will not necessarily feel the impact of climate change first. The effects will be borne mostly by the poorer nations who will be unable to pay for the flood defences and the import of food when their own arable land succumbs to some combination of drought, flood, salinity and loss of topsoil.

Growth economics not only fuels the richer nations' consumer lifestyles, widening the gap between rich and poor, but it is also responsible for increasing greenhouse gases in the atmosphere. There is a moral argument that the richer nations should already be doing more to help the poorer nations to alleviate starvation and poverty. Regardless of that, though, the message is clear – climate change is the concern of every individual, social organisation and government the Earth over.

Monbiot provides a target to avoid the worst effects of climate change. Referring to the latest IPCC projections he states that

> the only means... by which we can ensure that there is a high chance that the temperature does not rise to this point (two degrees) is for the rich nations to cut their greenhouse gas emissions by ninety per cent by 2030.

No doubt the denial industry would enjoy taunting Monbiot as hysterical and over-reacting. However, he is merely employing a logical process based on statements and conclusions. The statements of science are clear and Monbiot's conclusions logically follow. They are not merely expressions of sentiment. But still, it makes for fairly uncomfortable reading to think of ourselves as killers, even without intent. It leaves all of us in a difficult position. It is easy to retreat into our individual selves and like ostriches bury our heads in the sand hoping that it will all go away. The alternative would appear to be to tackle something that is so big that the task becomes an impossible and depressing burden. There is no doubt that Monbiot's statement is a challenge to the lifestyles of each and every one of us. But how is it possible to respond and lead a productive, meaningful and healthy lifestyle without making things worse?

Science alone cannot help with this question. Climate change is not just about facts, figures and targets. Although scientists have provided the evidence, the consequences of climate change relate directly to what we value. This is not so much about science as a response to risk, where the risk is to ourselves. Unless we see this then we will not begin to see what is at stake.

Who are we as a species living on this planet right now, and what does the threat of climate change mean for us and our futures? There may remain differing nuances around morality, values and ideologies but right now that is the ultimate question we need to address regarding human life and evolution.

A strong and vivid reminder of the fact that, as a society, we need to find ways of working with nature occurred as I approached the narrows at Caolas nan Con where another five-knot tide runs. I had purposely taken my time from the narrows at Ballachulish to allow the tide to turn, but as it happened I arrived a little early and the last of the outgoing stream was still quite strong. Utilising the following wind I raised the sail and with some hard paddling and the use of eddies I finally felt the grip of the stream easing as the narrows opened up. A strengthening tailwind meant that the last few kilometres into Kinlochleven amid the steep flanked hills of Aonach Eagach and the Mamores was simply joyful (see photo 8, plate section).

In high spirits I was pleased to see a smiling face welcome me. Jane had arrived to re-supply me with food and to transfer my notes from the 'AlphaSmart keyboard' I had with me onto a laptop. Since a major focus of my journey was to write this book I was concerned that my recording equipment might get wet and I would lose everything. Jane agreed to meet me at the end of each week to back up my notes. It was also good to spend time together and catch up. Having found a café we set up the AlphaSmart and the laptop to begin transferring data. Completely absorbed by lunch we both looked up to see someone playing with the keyboard on the AlphaSmart. With a surge of anxiety at the potential loss of data the man was confronted and asked to explain himself. It turned out that he had thought it was an interactive computer and part of the visitor display!

8

Learning outside the box

It is around six kilometres from the sea at Kinlochleven to the Blackwater Reservoir. For a canoeist to get there the problems are twofold. First, the reservoir sits at an altitude of three hundred and thirty metres above sea level. The second is that the River Leven, which connects the two bodies of water, is not navigable upstream in the same way that I managed to paddle, line, pole and wade up the rivers Ness and Oich. The gradient of those rivers was fairly even and gentle, but the Leven is characterised by narrow gorges and steep waterfalls. An ascent of the Leven, a river that kayakers consider to be grade five plus white water, would require all sorts of complicated technical climbing paraphernalia such as ropes, slings, karabiners and pulleys.

I decided instead to take the 'easy option' and follow the forest track marked on my map which runs roughly parallel to the river. This involved lashing my canoe onto a two-wheeled trolley and pulling it behind me in much the same way a skier hauls a

1. Starting at Inverness. (Photograph Jane Nicol)

2. Taking the canoe for a walk. (Photograph passer-by)

3. Entering Loch Ness.

4. Whitewater and deepwater paddles.

5. The passenger.

6. No tent required.

7. Poling.

8. When the wind fills my sail it fills my spirits too.
(Photograph Jane Nicol)

9. The long portage.
(Photograph Graham Harrison-Smith)

10. There must be easier ways of saving the planet!

11. My 'Yellow Brick Road'.

12. The navvy graveyard.

13. Forever unknown.

14. Blackwater dam.

15. Ascent of the Blackwater river.

16. Taking the strain.

17. Crossing peat hags.

18. Canoe resting on trolley: portaging the easy way.

19. The crannog at Eilean nam Faoileag.

20. The waterfall.

21. Another time!

22. Portaging the fish ladder.

23. One-eyed seal.

24. Pudding-shaped rock.

25. Humpback whale.
For an idea of its size note the A3 mapcase at its tail.

26. Me and my other shadow.
(Photograph Jane Nicol)

27. Homeward bound.

28. Wise elders.

29. A very long and steep storm beach.

30. The puffins: my guardian angels.

31. Jane joins me for the last leg.
(Photograph Barbara Duckworth)

32. One journey ends, another begins.
(Photograph Jane Nicol)

pulk. My three dry bags of luggage simply sat in the canoe. With some improvisation I tied my paddle onto the painter and used this as a harness. It acted as a yoke that I was able to loop over my shoulders.

Although my map showed a steep gradient I nevertheless expected a graded track fit for forestry vehicles. This was to be the longest portage on the trip and the longest time I would be away from water. I set out with high expectations of making good progress.

These expectations began to unravel quite quickly. The first sign that all was not well began almost imperceptibly – I had been working harder than expected pulling the canoe along the flat. At first I wasn't overly concerned because I still had fresh legs and was making good progress. However, at the first gentle gradient it began to dawn on me that I was still on the tarmac road and that pulling should have been much, much easier. Thinking about how I might struggle on the steeper sections I began to wonder if the wheels were running freely. Stopping to have a look I found that when I had tied the canoe onto the trolley I had failed to notice that there was little clearance between the canoe and one of the wheels. For the last four hundred metres the wheel had been rubbing against the side of the canoe. The fact that it had slowed me down meant little compared to the deep gash the sharp edges of the wheel tread had made in the plastic hull.

My first thought was that the trip was over. Although the wheel had not holed the canoe the gash was three or four millimetres deep and the inner material showed through. It was along the waterline, where I'd expect it to take some pounding from rocks later on when descending rivers. It looked as though even a slight collision would be enough to hole the boat. With some heavy white-water paddling ahead I wondered at the wisdom of proceeding with this canoe. The decision to continue was born of necessity because I did not have access to another nearby or at home.

I was much more careful when I retied the canoe onto the trolley and made sure there was a lot of clearance this time. Instant relief ensued with the wheel running freely and the task of pulling the canoe became much easier. With a greater sense of purpose I made my way past the processing plant of the British Aluminium Company's hydro scheme and smelter.

At last I began to make good progress. Even when the tarmac gave way to track the surface remained fairly even and progress was satisfactory (see photo 9, plate section). When the first significant gradient appeared I approached it with relish, since only a few minutes ago I had thought the trip over. However, as the gradient steepened progress became more painful. The canoe and I were having a tug-of-war. I would make a little progress and then the canoe, unfairly assisted by gravity, would begin inching backwards. I began resorting to some of the old military clichés I remembered: 'When the going gets tough the tough get going'. Well I didn't feel very tough, but common sense was telling me that the sandals I was wearing to let my feet breathe in the hot airless day were not the best footwear for the task.

Re-shod with stout walking boots that had a great deal more tread, I prepared myself for the next round of tug-of-war. With greater friction from my boots I could transfer more energy from my arms, chest, torso and legs through my feet to the towing of the canoe. However, power comes with a consequence and it wasn't long before the wheels came up against a small rock. In moving over it the canoe overbalanced and I had the first 'capsize' of the trip.

Convinced now that the tough had indeed got going I set about untying the upturned trolley from the canoe, removing all the baggage and retying everything back as it was. This took around fifteen minutes and I was soon inching forwards once more. By the time the first steep gradient levelled off I had a good rhythm going. As always, though, a sting in the tail awaits when you begin to feel superior to the task in hand. The next gradient was steeper than the last and the surface more uneven. Deeper wheel ruts and bigger and bigger rocks appeared. Not only was I straining against the incline but I had to slalom the canoe around large rocks and away from the deepest ruts.

It wasn't long before I had another capsize, and another, and another. I stopped counting after twelve. Strangely I was enjoying the physicality of the task. My forearms and back became sore with the pulling and the manual labour involved in propping up the canoe to slide the trolley under, and then having to retie everything. Although it was hard work and at times frustrating, generally speaking it seemed like honest work. But I was certainly tiring and I found myself taking frequent rests. During these I'd turn around and take immense satisfaction at the view of Kinlochleven slowly fading into the distance. In one of these contemplative moments I remembered seeing bananas beside the pile of food that Jane had laid out for me back in Kinlochleven. I began imagining all those squashed bananas inside my bags and the mess they'd be making of the rest of the food. Later that night I found no bananas and realised that they couldn't have been for me.

I could not believe my luck. On one of those numerous capsize occasions I stopped to adjust everything and there, lying on the ground beside the right hand wheel, lay the split pin that holds the wheel onto the axle. By coincidence I had stopped the moment it fell off. Had I continued a little longer the wheel would have fallen off and I doubt I'd ever have seen that split pin again.

With fortune smiling favourably once more I hunched forwards and took the strain, just as I heard behind me the faint sound of a high-pitched engine. As it grew increasingly louder I realised it was coming towards me and sure enough a trail cycle appeared and sped past me. It seemed that my self-righteous sense of honest labour and progress was being mocked by this noisy cheat. I thought of a few words that expressed my sentiments and muttered them under my breath. Worse was to follow when the motorcycle stopped at the top of the next gradient and the rider switched off the engine, removed his helmet and proceeded to watch me struggle up the hill. Inch by inch I approached the solitary figure and as I neared close enough to speak I was determined to seek and maintain the moral high ground. With as much humour as I could muster I asked jokingly if he had a tow-rope. 'Nut,' he said, kick starting the engine and driving off back down the hill.

Keen to make a little more progress before nightfall and with no prospect of a lift from the uncommunicative youth I continued with the struggle. With nothing else to think about I thought some more of our meeting. I wasn't surprised by what had happened. I could see that he was young, probably about seventeen. I reasoned that teenagers have got plenty on their minds dealing with hormones, never mind being civil to an older person. I imagined myself at that age and put myself in his shoes. I probably would have thought, 'What is that idiot up to, can he not get a lift from someone with an off-road truck?', as well as some far more uncomplimentary things. I was just beginning to think that I shouldn't attribute unkind sentiments to someone I did not know when I heard the sound of the motorbike again and returned to my initial character analysis. 'I bet he has brought his mates with him this time to gloat and goad me,' I mused.

Preparing for the worst I was relieved to hear the sound of only one motorbike draw near. He pulled abreast of me and stopped. He had a small rucksack on his back and took it off. As he reached inside he said, 'I've got a rope now.' The false stereotype I had created evaporated before my eyes and I felt a very strong sense of compassion for the young man. The idea of towing the canoe was utterly useless. I could see myself being showered with stones as they flew off the spinning back wheel. Also with greater horsepower than I could muster the incidence of capsize would increase. But it wasn't the relative merits of towing the canoe that occupied my mind. It was more to do with the emotion and feeling of what I was experiencing. We stopped for a while and chatted. I told him what I was doing and why and he told me about his love of biking. He knew these hills like the back of his hand, it seemed, and spent his summer evenings and weekends exploring them with his mates. He even had tips for me about where I should rest, where I should camp and how long it would take me to get to the reservoir. In this way we both shared our passions in life.

I continued on my journey humbled by the experience. I recognised passion in the young man and was reminded that it is a powerful emotion for someone wanting to do something in their lives. I knew too that this idea is key to harnessing human potential to act sustainably. If people's passions were directed more towards the importance of nature and our dependence on it then they could act as a powerful motivating force in our attempts to live sustainably.

I didn't have too much time to consider these things at the time because, in dribs and drabs, people began walking towards me. In singles, pairs, threes and fours they came, walking down the path. I was on part of the West Highland Way, one of Scotland's premiere long distance walking routes. Being late in the afternoon people were coming towards the end of their day's walk and looking forward to the final descent into Kinlochleven for their night's rest and most likely a well-deserved celebratory drink and meal. With this expectation the passing walkers were all in high spirits. I could see that most were completely bemused by seeing someone hauling a canoe up a boulder-strewn path that many were having difficulty walking down. From some distance away one group laughed loudly when they saw me and continued to do so as they passed. Another asked good-humouredly, 'Is the tide out?' Most, though, were curious and it felt good to get the chance to speak to them about the reasons for my journey.

My final encounter of the day began as I heard a vehicle approaching from up ahead. This being a narrow track there was no room for it to pass without me pulling the trolley off the road and onto the verge. As the verge was quite steep an overturned trolley appeared inevitable. I was relieved therefore when the driver saw me and started reversing into a passing place. Despite this kindness I was aware that he had no idea how slowly I was going – it would take me around ten minutes to get to where he was waiting. I resigned myself to dealing with an impatient driver. Sure enough the door opened and the driver got out. But he did not march angrily towards me. Without really asking about the absurdity of my situation he just went to the back of the canoe and pushed.

We stopped for a rest beside his beat-up old Range Rover. I knew without asking that by coming down the hill to help me he was not simply trying to get me out of his way. His was a genuine act of kindness. A gesture offered with nothing expected in return. We stopped and chatted for half an hour, even though he had other things to do. This was how I met Graham, who I would learn much from without him really teaching me anything at all.

He had lived for twenty years in a house half-way between Kinlochleven and the reservoir, with the track we were on really his extended driveway. I commented on the poor surface conditions of the track and Graham told me that severe storms and floods over the last few years had eroded it badly. It was in as poor a condition as he could remember. It turned out Graham was a sailor so we shared some adventures. He also told me some of the history of aluminium processing. Curiously, perhaps because he was a sailor, Graham was interested in the way I had tied the canoe onto the trolley. I could tell by the way he talked that he knew a better way to do it but was much too polite to say so. I also got the feeling that it would have been rude of me to ask him, perhaps he would feel uncomfortable being in a situation of superiority with knowledge I didn't have.

Graham left me with a suggestion for somewhere to camp and an invitation to stop at his house when I passed the next day. Until then I hadn't really thought about improving my tying-on system. Although the canoe kept overturning and the trolley slipping, I reasoned that the system was nevertheless working so I'd stick with it. I had originally tied the trolley immediately under one of the seats because this gave me a good attachment point. I started to experiment with moving the trolley further forward and using a thwart as a forward attachment point and the seat as a rear attachment point. Then the bags could be moved so as the balance point remained over the trolley wheels. By moving the trolley as little as a foot the stability of the canoe increased dramatically. For the rest of the portage the canoe did not overturn nor did the trolley slip its lashings.

Although the technical problem of adjusting the tie on point was solved this was not what occupied my mind. Graham's gentle manner of expressing his observations was a powerful stimulant for me to think more carefully about what I was doing. I guess people more thoughtful than I, or at least with a different way of thinking, would have adjusted the load and devised a more efficient method of towing and reduced the sweat, effort and physical labour much sooner. Still, Graham's gentle way was intriguing. A little later I arrived at the campsite that Graham had recommended, right next to a lochan set within birch tree woods – just beautiful.

The meeting with Graham affected me profoundly. I found myself concluding that it is not just what we learn but how it is learned, and that the *process* of learning is at least as important as the content. How, though, does this relate to the way in which we understand the relationship between humanity and nature? In communication terms it is clear that the environmental movement has tried to express its message, letting people know of the threats posed to the planet and its biodiversity – and then saying what we should and should not do. For example, used food and drink cans are a precious resource so the message is 'recycle them'. Long-line fishing for tuna is inadvertently responsible for hooking albatrosses so the message is 'stop buying tinned tuna'. Flying to exotic destinations increases carbon in the atmosphere so the message becomes 'reduce or stop flying'. The list continues. The point is that the message tells someone what to do or what not to do, and there is an implicit assumption, or hope, that people will act on it. This can be expressed in the simplest of equations: knowledge equals action. However, we know that this is not true because despite the threats to albatross and other seabirds long-lining still takes place and people still buy tinned tuna in the shops; despite the scientific consensus about climate change people are still flying; and despite strenuous efforts to recycle cans not everyone recycles.

So knowledge does not equal action, yet as a society we labour under this assumption. Part of the reason for this can be traced back to the industrialist epoch with the expanding British Empire and a corresponding growth in the capitalist economy. This global expansion of an empire where the sun never set required a massive investment in the sorts of trades and professions necessary to rule the empire. Key among these were engineers, planners, architects, clerks, medical professionals, politicians, diplomats and teachers. These professionals were trained within an education system through curricular subject areas such as mathematics, science, engineering, technology, languages, social studies and the arts.

Despite modifications to the curriculum throughout the industrial epoch the unspoken assumption then and now is that students are being prepared for a life within a society characterised by growth economics. An educational system that does not include itself as the subject of study has been allowed to proceed as though its subject areas of study are self-evidently good.

The argument I am putting forward is that schools and universities were, and still are, microcosms of global capitalism. However, if the purpose of education is to prepare students for their futures then, given the threats posed to humanity by climate change and other environmental issues, it would appear that the current education system is not fit for purpose. In response to these issues the influential Scottish educationalist

Professor John Smyth OBE has commented that 'it is difficult to avoid the conclusion that many have reached, that education should be largely recast'.

As Professor David Orr points out, one of the problems with indoor learning is that it can lead to the suppression of the feelings from which respect, curiosity, wonder and awe for the world beyond the class or lecture room grows. This is not a wholesale attack on school and university education so much as an appraisal of what might be better taught out-of-doors. However, it is a challenge to subject-based curricula because of the way it leads to divisions in the way pupils and students understand the world. There is a tendency, perhaps for institutional convenience rather than philosophical preference, to separate and compartmentalise strands of knowledge which are in fact related.

Brennan has referred to this as 'framework thinking' and it can prevent learners from seeing beyond the subject they are studying (e.g. physics or biology) to the ecosystem as a whole. This way of presenting knowledge operates at the expense of an integrated understanding of the world. What is required is joined-up thinking that draws on both the social and natural sciences where learning takes place indoors and out. This way it is possible to see nature not simply as a set of subjects but as a social ecosystem in which human beings and their impacts are more clearly understood. In this manner education would be transformed into one indivisible and interactive subject focusing on the political and socio-economic influences that affect ecological processes.

There is one further problem that needs to be highlighted. The industrialist teaching profession is built around one significant and enduring figure – the teacher. We have teachers who specialise in subject areas and naturally fit into the boxes Brennan talks of. They are relied upon by pupils to impart specialist knowledge. When knowledge is viewed in this way it is easy to see how teaching can become a mechanical function involving knowledge transmission, a formulaic function little different from topping up a mobile phone.

These problems can be summarised under four headings:
- Purpose
- Content
- Method
- Subject relationships.

There is a problem about the purpose of education
The educational establishment has been slow to respond to the challenges of the environmental crisis. This is hardly surprising as it tends to promote the existing norms, values and ideologies of mainstream thinking. These are based within an industrial carbon-dependent economy, so when a problem like climate change comes along education is not prepared to deal with it. Thus the educational response to climate change has so far been small and incremental; the social system itself is never really challenged. It is not just that the educational establishment is in denial of the planetary emergency, it is more that it does not know what to do about the implications of it. Meanwhile schools continue in their traditional role of knowledge transmission. In this way the theory of environmental problems is shared but the issue of how to mobilise society to adopt sustainable lifestyles remains problematic. This is not to deny the great efforts made by some individuals in some institutions so much as to say that the problem is systemic and the search for solutions lacks guidance throughout all levels of society.

The system continues unabated because the threat to society is not apparent to all its members. However, the threat is great and is exacerbated by an education system that has so far been peripheral and marginalised by those elements of society (namely the economy) which seek to maintain the status quo. There is a moral obligation for education in all its forms (professional and vocational, informal and formal, international and domestic, curricular and non-curricular) to actively engage in what is essentially a critique of industrial civilisation.

There is a problem with what is taught – content
There is nothing inherently wrong with what is taught in schools and universities; indeed, flicking through the prospectuses of any institution you will find a mouth-watering range of study opportunities. The challenge is to return to first principles. The most important question now is, 'What do people need to know to act as democratic citizens in a world characterised by the threats of environmental issues such as climate change?' Furthermore, 'What would a curriculum look like that focused on the future of humanity?' When the questions are posed this way it is clear that people need to know about soil science so that they know how their food is grown, its nutritional value and the effects of pesticides and herbicides. People need to know about the chemistry of the atmosphere so that they are aware of the changes that increased CO_2 brings about. They need to understand where energy comes from, how it is harnessed, its polluting effects and the alternatives to current modes of electricity generation.

Most importantly people need to understand the science of ecology so that they can see how all beings are related through food chains, food webs and nature's cycles. They need to understand ecology as the web of life with its interconnected strands. They need to understand the importance of biodiversity to the web of life, the effect that human beings have on that web, and how humanity is but an infant species in evolutionary terms.

Through the social sciences people need an understanding of the workings of economics and the effects of consumerism. People should study how businesses might co-operate to solve the environmental crisis and not just compete with each other in the market place. There is a need to study the role of social institutions such as schools, universities, NGOs, governments and community groups to understand their role in social change.

Because the environmental crisis affects different countries in different ways, people need to understand international issues such as debt and poverty as well as domestic issues such as trade and commerce. Issues such as animal welfare, peace and war also have a place in this. People need to have an understanding of politics and how to be involved in decision-making at community, national or international levels. For Professor David Orr this means that people should be taught in the ways of environmental literacy. The environmentally literate individual 'will have a blend of ecological sensitivity, moral maturity and informed awareness of ecological processes that would make him or her unlikely to contribute (at least consciously) to further degradation of natural processes at either individual or corporate levels'.

People should know these things as they set out on career paths, so that in time each profession or vocation is filled by people who have the knowledge and motivation to act, and can change their profession to act sustainably. Also, it is not enough to wait for tomorrow's generations to solve the problems of today's consumption. Action is required now by everyone in every walk of life.

There is a problem with how things are taught – method
If education is to be recast it is not just the content that needs to be considered but also methods of teaching. Take for example a stereotypical classroom situation where a pupil asks the teacher a question. There is a presumption that the teacher is able to answer the question. This position of superior knowledge is institutionalised throughout the whole education system. This works well in subject-based curricula where in most situations teachers can be expected to have superior knowledge to their pupils.

There is a problem with this method of teaching, though. The problem is that there is no formula available for how to live sustainably. There is no recipe book for the teacher to work with. While we have knowledge to suggest that as a species we are living unsustainably, it is true to say that we do not have the knowledge (or wisdom) to share about how to live sustainably. Teachers are therefore faced with a proverbial 'Gordian Knot'. As a lecturer myself I am faced with this problem. If I want to be a teacher in this area I have first to admit that I do not know with certainty how best to go about my teaching. But there is a logical conclusion to this point. If the need to teach in this area is overwhelming (it is), and if it is not clear how best to teach in this area (it is not), then it follows that the educational establishment needs to experiment with non-traditional approaches to teaching. Challenging as this may at first appear, just like Alexander the Great's cutting of the 'Gordian Knot', there is an answer, although it does require bold action. Teachers, and by teachers I mean everyone responsible for the learning of others, will need to step out from behind the position of having superior knowledge.

This superiority is effectively maintained when knowledge is theoretical and intellectual. The Scottish polymath Professor Sir Patrick Geddes (1854–1932) was one of the first people to make the link between environment, education and teaching. He believed that learning should apply to action and that action was born from learning. In other words the primary role of education was that it should have a practical output. He developed a holistic philosophy of learning based on the 'three Hs' of heart, hand and head. These respectively related to emotional, physical and intellectual learning, and importantly should proceed in that specific order. This was particularly observable in one of his famous sayings: 'As for art and music, so for nature; better no teaching than without the feeling of the subject.'

It is not that intellectual learning is such a bad thing. Indeed, it has provided surgeons with the necessary knowledge to perform triple bypass heart surgery and made it possible for astronauts to land on the moon. Extraordinary as those achievements are it is easy to miss the point. If sustainability is to be society's organising principle then it is fair to ask about the carbon emissions resulting from space exploration. In what way has space technology contributed to a more sustainable planet? Would the vast amount of money that has been used to fund such projects not have been better spent on projects such as flood defences? Why explore another planet when we are not yet able to look after our own? As for heart transplants, why do we wait until people's hearts and arteries are clogged up with plaque from eating unhealthy diets? If people paid better attention to diet and exercise there would be less need for heart transplants. A little preventative health education would be much better for the body than the prospect of invasive surgery that splits the chest open.

Facts alone do not provide an adequate understanding of how to be and act in the world. As the pioneering schoolmaster Cecil Reddie once said, facts 'can be got by any fool from encyclopaedias and works of reference; what matters is that you should learn to *think*'.

Geddes' motto was that 'by living we learn'. Education should not be a dress rehearsal for life so much as a way of identifying and dealing with life itself, with all its problems, promises and beauties. When looked at this way it follows that education should seek out real-life problems so that people can use their intellectual capabilities to solve them. Herein lies part of the solution. Those in society who are responsible for the teaching of others need to rethink current methods of teaching as they are not fit for the challenges ahead.

More experimental approaches to learning will open the door to conceptualising the main problems. Such approaches would not assume that method and content are the same things. When teachers step over this threshold what awaits on the other side are approaches such as problem-based learning and participative enquiry. In both these approaches the teacher is not an expert but a co-enquirer. Learners and teachers share their knowledge where the purpose is to solve problems. Of course there will always be a role, and a welcome one at that, for those with expert knowledge. However, since the primary goal of the exercise is action, the process is not complete when the expert passes on their knowledge, for example the knowledge to erect a wind turbine in a school ground, but when the co-enquirers have erected the turbine. These approaches already exist and can be seen in community approaches to issues. They are less evident in more formal institutions where much of society's education takes place.

There is a problem with the relationship between subject areas
There are two important aspects missing from what a reformed educational vision might look like. The first is to do with the curriculum. If the role of the teacher is no longer clear then who (or what) should guide learning? In any change process there is always an element of anxiety and so there will be concerns about how to link subject areas through co-operative enquiry. I think that all of this can be overcome by creativity and willingness from the educational establishment. I believe this because I know of the creativity and energy that already exists within the teaching profession and that could be directed towards this problem.

I remember once sitting by my tent on a two-thousand-metre col in the Pyrenees mountains enjoying the gathering dusk. All of a sudden a group of over a hundred swifts flew over just above my head. For me this was a magical occurrence. I had never seen such a large group of swifts flying together in a single direction. However, it was the noise that struck me as they passed only feet above my head. Similar to the noise a hand-held kite makes when twisting and turning through the air, the noise of these passing birds seemed disproportionate to their seemingly small individual bodies. I wondered at their purpose. I also wondered at their amazing ability to fly.

There remain many elements of this experience that I cannot explain to myself. I do not fully understand why it was so magical for me, yet it was at the time and remains so. Certainly I could rationalise the experience and attempt to explain it, but I know I could never do so fully. The explanation could never be the same as the experience. However, the inability to explain should not be seen as a weakness. Abstractions of reality (in this case language) are one step removed from that which it is supposed to represent. From an educational point of view it can provide inspiration to learn more. As a result of that single experience I came to read more about swifts and learned how to distinguish between swifts, swallows, house martins and sand martins. This in turn led me to investigate how the sightings of birds indicate seasonal change. At home I now listen for the first mistle thrushes singing from their treetop perches in February. In March I see flocks of lapwings, oystercatchers and black-headed gulls using the River Spey as a navigation handrail to find their way from their wintering grounds on the coast to the local farmlands where they will spend their summer. In April I know that the ospreys begin to arrive from Africa to nest in the Caledonian pinewoods all around my home, and so it goes on.

This was precisely the type of education that the American educational reformer John Dewey (1859–1952) believed in, where one experience was used as a basis for new experiences. From his perspective an experience was not a standalone event, it was the basis for other experiences. One learning episode should be linked to another, and another, and another. Many years later I still look for swifts on summer evenings. The incident sparked a lifelong interest for me. I do not expect this story to be magical for anyone else in the way that it was for me, but I hope that readers will have their own such instances to recollect. Theoretical learning, while extremely important, represents an incomplete form of knowledge. Providing joined-up experiences is one of the major opportunities of learning in the outdoors. Thus people can come to know the world not only through theoretical learning but from feelings of respect, curiosity, wonder and awe for the planet which sustains them. This opens the door to ways of linking inspirational experiences in the outdoors with the theoretical issues of sustainability that make sense to people's ordinary and everyday lives.

These ideas go a long way in describing why I was so influenced by my meeting with Graham. I had guessed that there was an answer to the problem of my overturning canoe. Graham could have taught me a better way but didn't. Although he did not teach me anything he inspired me to learn. The point is that when it comes to living sustainably, or anything else for that matter, it is not so much the transmission of knowledge that is important but the willingness to learn and act – and that cannot easily be taught.

9

Mind, matter and motorbikes

I WAS KEEN TO BE OFF EARLY THE NEXT MORNING. THE YOUNG man on the motorbike had told me that there was a Scottish Championship trials bike race and the first kilometre of my route would be on part of the circuit. I did not sleep well that night thinking of these speeding machines flying round a blind corner to find an overturned canoe in their path. Graham had told me the next stage was much steeper and much more rutted. He offered to drive me to the reservoir. I don't really think he expected me to say yes but I thanked him. Graham had seen how I had struggled on the lower section and did not believe I'd be able to make it up the next stage. He did say, though, that a cup of tea would be waiting if I arrived.

With the promise of a cup of tea, the challenge set by Graham's warning that I might not make it, and the threat of being run down by a motorbike, I set off in haste. Before long I understood Graham's predictions. The gradient was indeed steeper and the track more rutted. It was so steep that the road zig-zagged to make the gradient suitable for motorised vehicles. In addition piles of gravel ran like glacial lateral moraines down the line of the ruts deposited there by cascades of water from the last winter storm. Progress was painfully slow and, at times, I was going more backwards than forwards. It was clear that another approach was required, so I separated the canoe from the bags and shuttled the bags first and came back for the canoe. Leapfrogging like this was slow work but physically much easier. Just being able to make some progress was a relief. I remembered my diary note to describe the ascent of the day before – 'just short of brutal', which prompted a wry inward laugh. This section was even harder (see photo 10, plate section).

Nearing Graham's house I could hear the noise of revving motorbike engines in the valley below – the race had started. Two spectators walked past me, eager to get to a good spot to watch the action. Worried about my safety, as well as that of the riders, they offered to carry my bags the last two hundred metres. With the sound of motorbikes approaching at speed I had no second thoughts. Summoning all the energy I could muster I high-tailed it up the hill with the speedsters in close pursuit and rounded a bend to see Graham's house. I pulled into his drive with seconds to spare just as the first of the bikes roared by. Sweating profusely and completely worn out I sat down on the grass verge and howled with laughter at my crazy situation. There I was running (well, sort of) up a hill with a canoe on wheels being chased by a pack of motorcycles.

Graham's house is sat at an altitude of three hundred metres, two kilometres away from the nearest house along the heavily rutted track I had just ascended. Its garden was planted with daffodils, in full bloom as I arrived, but the birch trees were yet to show the signs of spring. The tea was very welcome and when Graham's partner Mary offered me a chocolate egg I remembered that it was Easter Sunday. I mentioned to Graham that I had been reading Patrick MacGill's book *Children of the Dead End*, an autobiographical novel of an Irish navvy who worked on the construction of the Kinlochleven hydro scheme and Blackwater dam. It is a riveting and graphic account of the hardship endured by the labouring underclasses during the late nineteenth and early twentieth centuries. Accidental explosions maimed and killed; poverty, alcohol abuse, theft, fighting and redundancy all loomed large in the everyday lives of the people.

Graham did not need much encouragement to quench my thirst for knowledge of his local landscape and brought out an album full of original photographs taken during the time of construction of the dam. The faded yellow pages seemed to add authenticity to the grainy images. We looked at what is now the bed of the Blackwater Reservoir, which just over hundred years ago was a village with two thousand people living in it. A whole transient community developed around the construction site with schools, shops and living accommodation. The foundations of the huts are still visible in front of and at the south side of the dam. Rumour has it that some houses existed to the north of the dam and now lie at the bottom of the reservoir, with the lapping waters hiding the secrets of those hardy people.

Graham showed me pictures of the conduit that draws water from the reservoir and delivers it to the smelter below. The water runs freely without any need for pumps. Hydrostatic pressure and gravity combine to create sufficient energy to operate the turbines below. I learned about German prisoners-of-war who built a concrete pipeline to take water from Loch Eilde Mhor to the Blackwater. The evidence of their labours are marked on the Ordnance Survey 1:50,000 map. They also built the road that links Kinlochleven and Glencoe. Graham showed me an old British Alcan brochure that has diagrams of the tunnels and waterways that link nearby Loch Treig with Loch Laggan and supplies water to the Fort William power house.

Graham's enthusiasm and knowledge of local history was absorbing and what started off as a cup of tea rapidly appeared to be merging with lunch. With greater resolve than I thought myself capable of I took my leave. Retracing my steps to the door I passed by photographs of the landscape I dared not look at. How easy it would have been to stay awhile. Graham had one last surprise for me, though, and pointed me towards the concrete conduit that he had mentioned earlier. 'Follow that,' he said, 'and it will take you all the way to the dam.' Following my previous exertions I could not believe my ears. With a little sun lighting up the concrete I was looking at my very own yellow brick road linking me to the Irish navvies and their sunken emerald city some four kilometres distant (see photo 11, plate section).

Just short of the dam lies a cemetery perched on a small knoll, whose inhabitants are contemporaries of Patrick MacGill. It is a strange cemetery, with headstones perched at odd angles and moss filling the criss-crossed weather cracks forming on the unpolished stone. The comforting uniformity of 'civilised' cemeteries is absent. There are no flowers, no beautifully adorned headstones, no manicured lawns and no maintained paths. The rocky and heathery landscape is as bare as it was when these people were interred. I paused at each headstone to pay my respects (see photo 12, plate section).

My gaze settled on one because the headstone bore no name. The date was 26/6/08, and it carried the disturbing inscription

'Not Known'. I sensed that something terrible had happened. This was probably the grave of a man who had laboured on the dam. It is possible that this person died of natural causes, perhaps because he was newly arrived at the construction site no-one knew his name. However, I know from McGill's accounts that it is very likely that his death was the result of an accidental explosion. I wondered if the reason he had no name was because his mangled remains could not be identified. Whatever the cause of death I mourned that there lay a person who died probably far from home with loved ones ignorant of his passing. Perhaps those loved ones never found out that he had died (see photo 13, plate section).

The majority of the workers were itinerant labourers driven from their distant homes in Ireland and Scotland by poverty. Some would send their money home to support struggling families while others just moved from job to job spending whatever they earned as they went. Despite the wonderful sight of the snow-clad peak of Buachallie Etive Mor I did not dwell. I continued along my yellow brick road and arrived at the dam twenty-four hours after leaving Kinlochleven (see photo 14, plate section).

I had thought of camping at the dam because of its remote setting and wonderful view of Kinlochleven far below. There was a spot in the lee of the dam protected from the wind and I was strongly tempted to stay there in a landscape full of stories I was becoming familiar with. I looked through the surface of the water and peered into its depths at where the sunken village would be, imagining its inhabitants going about their business all those years ago. I was reminded of the mythical Scottish village of Brigadoon that appears for one day every hundred years. It was ninety-nine years since the workers were buried in the cemetery, and a hundred years since people lived on the bottom of the reservoir. Maybe today would be the day that the village comes to life. Maybe then I'd have the chance to ask 'Not Known' his story.

The lure was strong but the call of the journey stronger. With another three hours of potential travel time and a following wind I looked out the sail in anticipation of starting down the Blackwater Reservoir's thirteen kilometres length. The wind was gusting around force five and reminded me of the near misses I had had before. If I had capsized then in what were relatively busy waterways there would have been a good chance of someone coming to my aid. Here I expected to see no-one and so I would have to be self-sufficient. I attached the rope from the sail to a thwart with a quick release knot but nevertheless kept my fixed blade knife handy in case of an emergency entanglement. The spare paddle was near to hand in case I accidentally let go of the one I was using and I made sure the bailer was by my side. It is not possible to roll my craft back upright as it would be with a kayak, and so before setting off I considered my options in the event of being capsized or swamped by waves. I only had two options really – either right the canoe and try to paddle it swamped to the side, or swim to the side without it.

Neither of those were great options so my message to self was 'don't capsize'. However, even in the lee of the dam I was having difficulty raising the mast because of the strength of the wind. All of a sudden, as I struggled to insert the mast through the hole in the thwart and into the masthead, the wind filled the sail with a loud crack and I was thrown to the rear of the canoe. The intermittent flapping of the sail tugged at the canoe, which responded like a bucking horse. I was relieved that my more experienced canoe friends were not there to see this pantomime. However, as I manoeuvred the canoe to bring the wind fully behind, the sail stopped flapping and with a constant wind filling it the canoe began to accelerate out into the open water. As long as the wind stayed behind and I was not turned sideways I figured I would be okay.

I had no idea what speed I was doing. The canoe was straining and creaking from the top of the mast through the sail to the canoe itself. I had my otter-tail paddle towards the stern, using it to steer and keep the wind behind me. After portaging the long, long rutted track, sailing gave the impression that I was proceeding with unseemly haste. The further I travelled down the reservoir the longer the fetch became and the bigger the waves. I could feel that familiar sensation of being picked up by a wave. As it passed under the canoe the stern began to rise and the bow lowered, allowing the canoe to accelerate down the front of the wave – I was surfing. Wave after wave surfed me further along the reservoir, and my whole being focused on keeping the canoe straight. There was little room for error. With no keel on my canoe I could be easily turned sideways to the waves; the lateral wind would make the craft very unstable and vulnerable to capsize. However, any thoughts of disaster were pushed to the outer recesses of my mind by the sheer exhilaration of moving at such a speed. Gathering clouds began to move in to obscure the hills either side of the reservoir. When they reached the loch the hills became completely hidden and without the perspective of depth I felt like a crash test dummy in a tunnel being propelled towards some impending collision. Bay after bay whizzed by and it was not long before I arrived at the end of the reservoir. With storm clouds gathering and rain threatening it was time to get the tent up and a brew on.

Heavy rain passed through during the night and by morning the wind had dropped, leaving me pleased to have made use of it when I could. Faced with more rain and the uninspiring prospect of hauling the canoe over eight kilometres of trackless moor I decided to catch up on my notes, read a bit and think. After the rigours of the ascent and exhilaration of the sail I was keen not to fall behind with the more contemplative side of my journey.

The Bible gives people dominion over the Earth and its other inhabitants, and the Industrial Revolution reduced nature to resources to fuel the economy's need for growth. Even the way we think has had an enormous influence in the way we relate to nature. Mud is dirty, spiders scary, sharks and lions become 'man-eaters' and so on. Almost unconsciously over time we have found a place for ourselves that keeps nature at a distance. Our homes, schools, factories and offices are all designed to keep nature out and us in. This does make some sense because computers do not work in the rain, paper gets blown away and manufacturing systems often need to be temperature controlled. The infrastructure required for this indoor lifestyle is understandable but whatever the arguments for and against it are there is one consequence that is inalienable. The vast majority of people living urban-based industrial lifestyles are well and truly insulated from the rhythms of nature. Humanity has become disconnected from nature.

Sitting in my tent with the rain beating down I felt very happy to be insulated from nature. I am not suggesting that we should empty offices and factories and return to a hunter-gatherer way of life. I am more interested in what happens when the layers of civilisation are removed. This does not amount to physically dismantling society, rather to understanding the world as it currently is so we can consider the one we'd like to have in the future.

Some philosophers use the technical word 'ontology' to refer to what might in everyday terms be thought of as a worldview, standpoint or a foundation. In other words it is the basis from which thoughts about the world are formed around. Ontologies are based on patterns of beliefs about the world and they are the foundations on which cultures develop, values are formed and how in turn people go about their daily lives. An example might help to explain. If someone believes in a God then it may well influence them to go to a place of worship (church, mosque synagogue) and to pray. Belief in the existence of a God is an ontological assumption and this belief has become codified in society through the development of religions which have rules of inclusion and expectations of its followers. The Enlightenment, the Romantic period and Marxism are all examples of ways in which societies throughout history were influenced by very different ways of thinking about the world.

The first point to be made is that the way we relate to the world has never been in a fixed state, rather it is part of a fluid process that changes over time. Environmental philosophers have, over the last fifty years, been attempting to work out why existing ontologies do not fully account for the current environmental crisis and the future existence of humanity. It is fair to say that there is no single ontology that offers a full explanation. However, one ontological assumption I would like to explore is that 'humanity is inseparable from nature'.

When written like that or spoken quickly, this very short sentence does not seem to amount to much. But think for a minute about the statement, 'I believe in God'. Great acts of both kindness and cruelty have been done in God's name. Wars continue to be fought and missionaries continue to preach in God's name. Beliefs can indeed be powerful motivations for actions. So what does the belief that humanity is inseparable from nature really mean?

The first thing to note is that it is a fairly straightforward biological fact because our own survival depends on clean air, clean water and nutritious food. The corollary of this is that if humanity causes harm to nature it causes harm to itself. For example, industrialism has already changed the composition of the atmosphere and if it continues to do so the atmosphere will be unfit for human life. David Suzuki says that 'the interconnectedness of all things on Earth means that everything we do has consequences which reverberate through the systems of which we are a part'. In other words we cannot be disconnected from nature because we are nature (even though we don't always acknowledge it).

So now there is a problem because on the one hand Suzuki is saying that we are infinitely connected with nature and on the other I am saying that society acts as though we are not. Herein lies the problem because appearances are indeed deceptive. Before looking at this idea of deception let us review some of the societal issues that have brought us to this point.

Despite the acceptance of governments throughout the world that sustainability is important, one of the main stalling points is translating its principles into practice. At the moment there is a gap between governments and the general public – people's everyday lives often mean that they remain disconnected from these issues, either unwilling to act or not knowing what to do. Until very recently this was understandable given the lack of political will and the belief that climate change was the fantasy of environmental fundamentalists. Now climate change is on the agenda of just about every political party in every industrialised country. So while the political consensus continues to develop at a strategic level, the concept of sustainability remains conceptually vague at grass roots level where individuals question how it affects them and what they should do about it. The majority of people now accept the ontological position that humanity is inseparable from nature, but they do not act as though they believe this. In summary, the problem of sustainability is now widely recognised but solutions are not so forthcoming.

Perhaps the gap between knowledge and action is to do with this idea of disconnection. Environmental philosophers tell us that experiences in the outdoors are particularly suited to exploring the people–nature relationship because an encounter with landscape is based on direct experience of it. A group of researchers has found that experiences in landscapes, such as fascination with flora and fauna, are foundational to how people live and act in later life. Professor Anthony Weston states that 'it is our sensory immersion that most profoundly links us to the land'. The touches of a raindrop or sunray are the most expressive ways of feeling warmth or cold. It is at this point that people are closest to nature and well placed to begin to understand the systems that make it work.

This fits in well with Geddes's idea of heart, hand and head. As we have seen, knowledge does not equal action, which explains why society knows there is a problem with the climate yet individuals remain immersed in a consumer lifestyle. What would happen therefore if 'the heart' as influenced by nature experiences were to be given more opportunity to express itself? How would this influence the false equation that knowledge equals action?

In a world where emotions are not supposed to get in the way of good judgement this may at first appear a perilous proposition – but it is not. In most cultures around the world people would not think of entering into a relationship with someone they did not know. This is particularly so in an intimate relationship such as marriage, which develops over time and involves qualities such as love and respect (this example is not intended to offend cultures that practice arranged marriages!). Such relationships can also be very hard work for the individuals involved. To succeed they require among other things commitment, tolerance, patience, forgiveness and understanding. In short we have a highly developed sense of what is required if human relationships are to be nurtured even if at times they are hard work.

This highly developed sense of relationship-building is spectacularly absent from the relationship that most of humanity currently experiences with nature. Because of our modern lifestyles we do not spend enough time getting to know nature and, more importantly, develop feelings for it. We do not base our relationships with other people on theoretical knowledge alone. Feelings and emotions are the glue that holds relationships together. Implicit in these ideas is that knowledge about sustainability, although extremely important, is not in itself a sufficient precondition to act sustainably. What appears to be missing is an emotional engagement or feeling of attachment with nature.

Part of the problem here is that we have been culturally conditioned to think of knowledge and feelings as being quite distinct. However, as educational philosophers and researchers such as Bloom, Krathwohl and Masia, have pointed out, 'the fact that we attempt to analyse the affective area separately from the cognitive is not intended to suggest that there is a fundamental separation. There is none'.

Inherent in this position is that there are more ways of knowing than just rational, cognitive or theoretical. The American psychologist and professor of education at Harvard University, Howard Gardner, explains this in his theory of multiple intelligences. His theory is based on the acknowledgement that traditional notions of intelligence such as cognitive and theoretical knowing do not account for the broad range of human potential. His theory was developed not simply in order to describe the world but as a method for changing it. Gardner describes his ideas thus:

Linguistic intelligence – involves sensitivity to spoken and written language and the ability to learn languages.

Logical-mathematical intelligence – involves the capacity to analyse problems logically, carry out mathematical operations, and investigate issues scientifically.

Musical intelligence – entails skill in the performance, composition, and appreciation of musical patterns.

Bodily-kinesthetic intelligence – entails the potential of using one's whole body or parts of the body (like the hand or the mouth) to solve problems or fashion products.

Spatial intelligence – features the potential to recognise and manipulate the patterns of wide space (those used, for instance, by navigators and pilots) as well as the patterns of more confined areas (such as those of importance to sculptors, surgeons, chess players, graphic artists, or architects).

Interpersonal intelligence – denotes a person's capacity to understand the intentions, motivations and desires of other people and, consequently, to work effectively with others.

Intrapersonal intelligence – involves the capacity to understand oneself, to have an effective working model of oneself – including one's own desires, fears and capacities – and to use such information effectively in regulating one's own life.

The fact that these intelligences have been characterised in this way is a good indicator that we can no longer think of education as simply the transmission of knowledge. Neither can knowledge be seen as something singular and theoretical in its nature. The theory of multiple intelligences demonstrates that there is diversity in both our thoughts and feelings.

More recently Gardner has suggested there are even more forms of intelligence, one of which is extremely important to the ontological position that humanity is inseparable from nature. He calls this 'naturalist intelligence', where individuals develop expertise in the recognition and classification of numerous species. It is also where humanity has the capacity to be comfortable in, and captivated by, the world of organisms. Furthermore he states that 'just as most ordinary children readily master language at an early age, so too are most children predisposed to explore the world of nature', a clear indication that they can be as happy outdoors as they appear to be in front of a television or computer screen.

Reading this description of naturalist intelligence I cannot help thinking of my own encounters with the Mycetophild on Loch Ness, or the swifts in the Pyrenees, and how each encounter inspired me to learn more. Importantly, this need not just be restricted to the biosphere. It was the same captivation with the geology of the Great Glen that inspired me to read more about it. For the hydrosphere, I recall the captivating effect of looking down Loch Ness when the sky was reflected back to me from the depths of the loch. As for the atmosphere, what could be more captivating than the amazing sights of the aurora borealis?

The rain showed no signs of abating so I resolved to break camp and start the crossing of Rannoch Moor (see photo 15, plate section). The first problem I encountered was that the river I had hoped to pole or line at least part of the way was too dry. Large round boulders lay strewn across the river, making any upstream passage impossible. Unfortunately I had not really thought about how to portage the canoe and equipment. Looking out across the moor I could see an expanse of heather and hummocks. There was no track to follow, rendering my trolley useless. I tried dragging the loaded canoe but it was too heavy. I improvised a harness and used it to drag the canoe but still I made little progress. I resigned myself once again to carrying the bags forward and then coming back for the canoe. By experimenting with different ways of improvising a harness I found that the best way was to wear my buoyancy aid the wrong way round. It had a large back pocket which I normally kept a throw rope in. This created a bulge and with a loop tied onto the painter I rested it on the bulge around chest height. It was a good height for me to lean into and take the strain (see photo 16, plate section).

The next problem I had to resolve was how to navigate over the moor. The rounded knolly terrain presented certain technical problems, particularly as the mist obscured visibility. It would be easy to take a bearing to where I wanted to go, but it would leave me little chance to deviate if I wanted to miss a particularly large knoll. Making use of a small-scale map (1:50,000) left me open to encountering obstacles on the ground not shown on the map. I could ascend a knoll that was 9.999 metres high then descend into a depression 9.999 metres deep on the other side and not know it from the map alone. In normal walking conditions the unaccounted-for height difference would be fairly insignificant, but it would represent a substantial obstacle for me pulling a canoe.

Even with the mist down I was not concerned about becoming lost as there were plenty relocation strategies available. The main one was the railway line that ran at right angles to my direction of travel – even if I were to get disorientated I just needed to keep heading in its general direction. As soon as I reached it all I would have to do was turn right and follow it to Rannoch Station. Given these variables I figured that the best route choice was to follow the course of the river. Because of the meanders this would make the distance of travel much longer but I reasoned it would be worth it for not having to steadfastly follow a bearing over knolls and depressions. I could also cut across some of the bigger meanders shown on my map.

No sooner had I set off than I felt justified in the route choice because, for most of the time, grass and moss ribbon lined the riverbank. This was far easier terrain to drag a canoe over than heathery, rocky knolls. Although progress was slow I knew I could keep going all day and the next if required – just as well at a rate of four hours per kilometre and a half.

I was reminded of the variety of ways in which the Inuit people manage to navigate their sea kayaks over long distances. One of those was by knowing where the prevailing wind comes from and all its subtle variations as it weaves its way through the hills and valleys of the landscape. For me the wind was coming from the west, and as long as it stayed at my back I knew was heading in the right direction. That was important because there were tributaries along the river. I could easily mistake one for the main river and end up walking the wrong way.

These portages were not the best part of my journey but neither were they the most unpleasant. There was something rewarding about it, and despite the physical effort I began to think of it as a rest day. Although it was not restive in the sense that it remained hard work, it was a rest day for my forearms and wrists, which I needed to be in good shape to finish the journey.

The internationally renowned philosopher and psychoanalyst Erich Fromm challenged the view that life is or should be easy. The notion of an effortless life, he believed, could be traced back to, among other things, industrialist technology which 'diminished the amount of physical energy necessary for the production of goods'. He continues:

> This liberation from hard work is experienced as the greatest gift of modern 'progress'. And it *is* a gift – provided that the human energy thus liberated be applied to other, more elevated and creative tasks. However, this has not been the case. The liberation from the machine has resulted in the ideal of absolute laziness,

of the horror of making any real effort. The *good* life is the *effortless* life; the necessity to make strong efforts is, as it were, considered to be a medieval remnant, and one makes strong efforts only if one is really forced to do so, not voluntarily. You take your car to the grocery store two blocks away in order to avoid the 'effort' of walking...

I can relate to Fromm's idea that there is no promised land of painless existence. Understanding that is central to the journey towards sustainability because, if nothing else, it involves a lot of hard work, physically, mentally and emotionally. But there is hope implicit in Fromm's analysis because what he is saying is that hard work is rewarding. Not only that but as a species it is what we have been used to throughout the hunter-gatherer and agriculturist past. It is just that we have forgotten this in the last few hundred years.

Rannoch Moor was living up to its reputation of being wet overhead, wet underfoot, and bleak. Yet it has its own beauty. As the cloudy showers passed through a little sun emerged from the clouds to gladden the landscape. At the top of knolls I scanned the landscape for signs of the watershed where I would begin dragging the canoe downhill instead of uphill.

To keep the portage interesting, and with deep ditches and peat hags to cross, I set myself fun challenges. The task was to find ways of crossing gaps too wide for me to step over. One tactic I developed was to take the canoe to the edge then lean out to test the friction and find the point of balance. I would then take a step backwards to provide some slack for me to take a leap strong enough to free the canoe and propel me to the other side of the hag. The critical factor was judging the slip/friction of the canoe to perfection, otherwise one of two things would happen. To bottle it at the last second meant being rammed from behind by the canoe. Alternatively, if I took off having misjudged the slip/friction, the rope would tighten in mid-air, leaving me to fall into the mire below. Boldness came with practice and I found myself attempting some of the hags by running at them, taking a wild leap and leaving the rest to chance (see photo 17, plate section).

Suddenly a rainbow appeared in front and by some divine coincidence led me to the watershed at Lochan a Chlaidheimh. It had taken eight hours to cross three linear miles from the Blackwater Reservoir. The moment was not lost on me. At an altitude of three hundred and fifty metres I was at the highest point of the journey and every centimetre above sea level had been gained under my own steam. From now on it would be downhill all the way to the North Sea.

There is more to this exploration of intelligences. What Gardner's theory helps to explain is that our intelligences are much more complex than so recently thought. While the importance of emotional learning is recognised there is much more to it. Gardner discusses thinking about feelings. In this sense 'feelings' remains a conceptual notion, something still an adjunct to cognitive thought. More recently there has emerged a greater scientific basis to explain the relationship between Gardner's presentation of intelligences and how emotions fit in. Modern developments in neurobiology, such as brain imaging, have provided greater detail on the origins of emotional intelligence and how emotions affect our behaviour. The internationally acclaimed psychologist Daniel Goleman points out that, 'like the kinesthetic realm, where physical brilliance manifests itself nonverbally, the realm of the emotions extends, too, beyond the reach of language and cognition'.

The point here is that it is not cognitive intelligence that provides the motivation for human actions (which firmly puts to the sword the idea that knowledge equals action). The emotions we experience are responsible for behaviour. Here we arrive at the crux of understanding why, despite the knowledge we already have about sustainable lifestyles, we remain largely passive in our actions.

It is important to note that emotional learning is not anti-intellectual, nor is it simply about pandering to people's whims and fanciful notions. Like any learning, for most of us, it is hard work. As Goleman says, with effort, emotional learning becomes ingrained

as experiences are repeated over and over, the brain reflects them as strengthened pathways, neural habits to apply in times of duress, frustration, hurt. And while the everyday substance of emotional literacy classes may look mundane, the outcome – decent human beings – is more critical to our future than ever'.

What Gardner and Goleman show is that when it comes to learning, people are not being challenged to the fullest of their capacities (cognitive or emotional). Furthermore, cognitive learning does not take place in isolation from feelings. It is the qualities associated with being outdoors for prolonged periods that provide opportunities for being immersed in nature and the thoughts and feelings that result. These experiences are largely absent from the everyday life of industrialised humanity.

10

The hidden connection

As I packed away my tent I became aware of a presence behind me and looking around saw something moving through the heather. Rubbing my newly opened eyes for a better view I saw it was the Fort William to Glasgow train on the track I had forgotten was there. Knowing that this was no metaphysical apparition did nothing to dispel my initial sense that a train emerging from the early morning mist on a track hidden by heather was somewhat surreal.

Since the train was heading in my direction of travel I set off in hot pursuit. Pursuit does of course imply a degree of relativity but dragging a canoe downhill is much faster than dragging one uphill, and the feeling of speed was sufficient to keep my spirits high for the whole morning it took me to arrive at Rannoch Station. In my brutish attempts to drag the laden canoe I had managed to pull a muscle in my back and was doing my best to ignore the pain. My mind was angry with my body because of its injurious tendencies, and although I do not usually approve of masking pain symptoms by using drugs the disobedient back needed to behave and perform. Two painkilling and anti-inflammatory tablets helped my back see the error of its ways for a while longer.

When I arrived at Loch Laidon the wind was blowing hard once again. I set off into a force five headwind, looking for the entrance to the river called Garbh Ghaoir. On the map the entrance looked wide enough that finding it should not present any problems, so I packed my map eager to be on my way. Progress was painfully slow. I could not line as the wind was coming from the wrong direction and just pushed the canoe onto the shore. Poling was no good because my wrists were too sore so paddling was the best remaining option. In theory this should not have been too difficult because the river mouth was less than a kilometre away. However, it proved to be the hardest wind I had canoed into so far. Gusts were catching the nose of the canoe and spinning me round. Nevertheless I did make progress, but in the process lost touch with how far I had come. After an hour or so of intense effort I knew that I should have seen the river entrance so I landed to sort things out. With time to look at my map I could see from the contours that I had come too far. Walking up a small knoll I looked back to see the Garbh Ghoir glimmering invitingly in the sun – it certainly hadn't glimmered to me as I passed it by!

Now that I'd found it I recognised another problem. The recent dry spell meant that water levels were very low. The river was full of rocks with little flow to cover them. To make progress I had to scrape, hop, paddle and pull the canoe down-river, with the canoe getting trashed against the abrasive rock. There was evidence of others who had suffered the same experience and I followed their trail of red polyethylene on the rocks. I paddled as much as possible but the wind, which was behind me, played havoc with my ability to steer. Every time I set the canoe up to perform a delicate manoeuvre the wind gusted and changed my direction. On many occasions I ended up broached on rocks and cursed my clumsiness.

With great relief I navigated the three-kilometre rock garden that was the Garbh Ghoir and arrived at Loch Eigheach. Jane met me there for another re-supply and spent a night camping with me. She had brought Farril, our pet Labrador, which was part of the plan. However, she also brought two other dogs to help out a friend on holiday. With growing anxiety I realised that Jane had yet another plan. Three dogs were going to spend the night with us in our tent. With pulled muscles in my back, sore wrist tendons and painful forearms, my tent was about to be invaded by a pack of hounds. Jane had thought this through though and brought me some beer as a peace offering – she knows me well.

The ideas of Gardner, Goleman and Orr open a path to understanding the relationship between humanity and nature in a holistic way that includes not only cognition but emotional intelligence. However, what might the trigger be that could spark emotions powerful enough to curb levels of consumerism? To start with it is important to establish that, as Ryle says,

> there are two quite different senses of 'emotion' in which we explain people's behaviour by reference to emotions. In the first sense we are referring to the motives or inclinations from which more or less intelligent actions are done. In the second sense we are referring to moods…of which some aimless movements are signs.

This is an important distinction because it is essentially the difference between needs and wants. As we have seen in previous chapters, growth economics has been spectacularly successful in exploiting that aspect of human desire that can only be satisfied by buying more. The irony of this is that desires are never satisfied in any way other than temporarily and the elusive pursuit of happiness continues. This is what Ryle is referring to as 'aimless movements'. They are whimsical emotions which, far from providing satisfaction, tend to engender a desire for even more. Retail therapy and conspicuous consumption are both examples of the attempt to satisfy superficial emotions. Meantime the deeper emotions that Ryle describes as 'motives or inclinations' (needs) lie dormant, perhaps even suppressed. Not only that but because the pursuit of happiness is fundamental to each of us the superficial pursuit of consumerism comes to be thought of, wrongly, as 'motives and inclinations'. Thus needs become confused with wants. This is an important point because society has more of an obligation to provide for people's needs than their wants.

Loch Eigheach is part of a hydro-electricity scheme. At its eastern end a dam separates it from the River Gaur. As there was minimal outflow from the dam, canoeing the four-kilometre stretch would not be easy. Water levels were very low and there were no clear deep-water channels. Reminded of the Garbh Ghaoir frustrations I noted with interest that my map showed a tarmac road which followed the line of the river. I lashed the canoe to the trolley and set off to experience a different sort of adventure as cars passed by with only inches to spare. I laughed in the face of danger, happy that for the first time on the trip I was doing a trolley portage downhill on a smooth surface. I had the pleasant choice of either having to slow the speed of the canoe on the steeper downhill sections or run fast enough to keep up with its momentum (see photo 18, plate section).

The sun was pleasantly warm and with the quick progress my spirits soared. A young guy about fifteen years old cycled past and asked if I needed help, I said I was coping and he said, 'Ach cool'. It seems that in life kindness and aid is never far away, even though at times it doesn't always seem that way.

A bridge at Rannoch Barracks where the river ran deeper provided a suitable place to re-launch the canoe. With a gentle tail wind and the sail raised, Loch Rannoch opened up and I headed for the crannog at Eilean nam Faoileag. It is a stone-built island with most of its ancient construction submerged since the two-metre rise in water level following the construction of Loch Rannoch dam. A nineteenth-century tower is virtually all that remains to be seen (see photo 19, plate section).

With a gentle tailwind creating only small waves, the sail kept me ahead of the breeze. The canoe followed in a windless peacefulness. I had nothing to do but steer and relax, allowing the warming sun to add to my contentment. A sea shanty came to mind, as sung by Davy Steele on the Battlefield Band's album *Rain, Hail or Shine*.

> Man your boats and leave the whale
> What care we for calm or gale
> Aye tak a drink as long as you can
> Brandy's guid amongst het ale
>
> Heave ya ho and away we go, heave ya ho and away-o
> Heave ya ho and away we go, heave ya ho and away-o

A folk song from the Scots tradition, it was sung by boatmen to help them row at the same speed in order to keep their net tight and even. But songs serve another purpose. Songs are themselves historical archives. They are part of, as Gardner points out, a form of intelligence. Like any written history book folk songs are mirrors reflecting the past. Singing them brings the past alive and provides a source of inspiration to learn more about history, culture and landscape.

If emotional literacy is to be nurtured, the first challenge is to penetrate beyond the superficiality of whimsical consumer-led behaviour. To do this involves an exploration of inner reality (what psychologists call self-awareness). The second is to explore what sorts of experiences spark deeper emotions and trigger actions consistent with the development of sustainable lifestyles. This involves an exploration of outer reality (the 'hidden' connections that link humanity and nature).

The ancient Greek philosopher Socrates is often credited with the saying 'know thyself know the world'. The starting point therefore in understanding the relationship between humanity and nature begins with the self, both you and me and every other individual on the planet (I do not want to suggest that the needs of those with affluent lifestyles are the same as those in poverty and so my focus remains on individuals living in industrialised countries and their consumerist lifestyles).

We have already seen how people consume things, go on exotic holidays and buy flashy cars to fulfil their needs (which are actually wants). This all appears part of a universal quest to find happiness. The problem is that the pursuit of happiness through consumerism is the basis of unsustainable lifestyles. I would like to propose one way of treading lightly on the planet that is very simple. Spend more time outdoors. This is because the outdoors is a place of beauty, exercise and a source of inspiration to learn all sorts of things. However, not much thought has been given as to how the outdoors might provide a way in which to understand the issues of sustainability. Take, for example, this journey. By anyone's definition it is an adventure. Yet climbers in this country see a progression from climbing in England's Lake district, to Scotland's higher mountains, to climbing in the Alps culminating in the ultimate challenge of climbing the so-called 'Greater Ranges' of the Himalayas. Canoeists too seek similar challenges in exotic places. The quest for such adventures is part of a consumerist culture where experiences become collectable items. Without necessarily saying that people should not be flying to exotic places for their holidays and adventures I am wondering if in many cases happiness cannot be found closer to home, where the environmental costs of travel in terms of GHG emissions are much reduced.

So the challenge is not just about spending more time outdoors, but spending more time outdoors in places nearer to where we live. Although I have called this journey *Canoeing around the Cairngorms* it is in fact a circumnavigation of my home. During the thirty-day journey I will never be further than ninety miles from my home and for most of the journey less than seventy miles.

Indeed, by some accounts the radius of my journey is extravagant. The North American environmental philosopher Henry David Thoreau said:

> there is in fact a sort of harmony discoverable between the capabilities of the landscape within a circle of ten miles' radius, or the limits of an afternoon walk, and

threescore years and ten of human life. It will never become familiar to you.

In other words to get to know an area well in your lifetime you need look no further than ten miles from your home. What awaits is a lifetime of adventures in your own backyard. To do this one needs to be able and willing to look for the extraordinary in the ordinary.

When you look at places the way Thoreau saw them, they are not merely playgrounds for the leisured classes. You find the extraordinary through employing the wider set of intelligences that Geddes, Gardner and Goleman have alerted us to. Not merely as passive observers but, as Thoreau said, by living 'deliberately' in them. By living deliberately in places, you choose to be in that place and not somewhere else.

When you see the landscape as Thoreau did you do not look in one direction to see biology, in another to see history, and in yet another to see chemistry, as the school timetable suggests. What you see is the curriculum unfolding as you pass through the landscape. The landscape is not reduced to convenient (or perhaps inconvenient) units of study but appears as it exists, as an integrated whole. In this way you come to know nature in a more holistic way, characterised by direct experiences of it. Any necessary theory is directly relevant to the experience. I did not, for example, know the life-cycle of the swift until I returned home and looked up the necessary information in a book. The heart, hand and head come together when related to direct encounters with landscape.

It is important to remember that landscapes are not just about rural places. Since the majority of people live in urban areas their places are important too. As Orr says, 'Place is defined by its human scale: a household, neighbourhood, community, forty acres, one thousand acres'. When you see the landscape this way it is not simply a backdrop for leisure activities, somewhere to build houses and factories or somewhere to dispose of rubbish. Instead intimate knowledge of places is the beginning of understanding our connection with and dependence on the Earth's systems.

The journey that allows us to travel outwards also helps us to travel inwards. It is here that a sense of personal intimacy with the landscape (rural and urban) can encourage a social identification with it. It is not sufficient to just be in a place. Instead it is important to be actively involved in learning about it. In this way the landscape becomes a part of who we are. Yes, we can play in it and build on it but we can also speak of it and act for it because it is an extension of ourselves.

Thinking of human identity in this way may at first appear rather abstract, perhaps even strange – but it is not. To see the truth in this we need only think of how some people already relate to places. Someone who comes from London is affectionately known as a Londoner, and if that Londoner happens to live within the sound of the Bow Bells they are proud to be known as a Cockney. People from certain cities will support certain football teams. One city may have two football teams and the fans' sense of identity is likely to be much stronger because of the geographical closeness of their rivalry. Through accents, stories, songs, histories and other shared experiences these identities are profoundly important to those who keep them alive. That is why the idea of identity in this context is not abstract. It is already being played out in the everyday lives of people across the planet.

It is this sense of identity that is absent in our relations with nature. As individuals within industrialised nations we tend to know it more theoretically than experientially. Nature is on the other side of a window, preserved in a museum, or something 'over there' and 'out there'. It is hard to envisage what a place-based identity with landscape might look like because we have to imagine it instead of living it. Here, therefore, we see the barrier between the inner and outer landscape. We naturally relate to what is around us but we cannot relate easily with the wider landscape because of our lack of contact with it. The everyday reminder of what makes a Cockney a Cockney or football fan a football fan is much, much stronger than our everyday identification with places and nature. When it comes to identification with these places we are essentially displaced people.

We now arrive at an interesting juncture. In order to better understand the relationship between humanity and nature I have suggested there needs to be an integration of multiple intelligences, emotional literacy, environmental literacy and a greater empathy for places local to our homes. Yet there is still a large piece of the jigsaw missing. In fact it is not just one piece, it may more properly be thought of as the outer edges of the jigsaw – a whole framework. The framework relates to the ideas about ontology and standpoints discussed earlier. It is to do with the sorts of values that nurture such a way of being in the world. We are missing a framework of morality that guides personal and societal decision-making towards sustainable lifestyles.

Another portage was required around the dam at the east end of Loch Rannoch and on to Dunalastair Water. The river was a mass of tree-clad islands and if it wasn't for the current that indicated my direction of travel it would have been easy to get lost. As the river opened out into the loch a curious and haunting site appeared. Trees were everywhere but their roots and lower trunks were submerged. Despite the tree cover being semi-natural the landscape had the appearance of a swamp, an uncharacteristic feature of the post-glacial Highland landscape. The loch now forms a modified habitat designated as a statutory Site of Special Scientific Interest (SSSI). Despite its scientific value and its obvious beauty it has the appearance of a drowned landscape.

The artificial reservoir narrowed as the hills closed in from both sides and another spectacular landscape opened up. Mature pine and alder tress perched precariously on the steep cliffs that enveloped me. I knew from the map that the mouth of the River Tummel was close. The steep-sided hills that converged from left and right acted as a tell-tale sign of a gorge ahead and a reminder to be careful. Major white-water challenges lay before me.

Heeding the warning I pitched my tent and took a walk downstream to inspect what the Ordnance Survey map marked as a waterfall. I had not paddled this stretch of river before and I didn't have a guidebook with me to indicate what was to come. However, I did know the river by reputation and knew that I was looking at a grade five fall. In the calm of the still evening air I imagined myself canoeing it, looking for the line I would take. In reality there was no safe line – my canoe would quickly swamp. Burdened by a canoe acting like a submarine I would be completely at the mercy of the immense power of the water. If I lived, died or was injured it would not be because of any particular canoeing skill I possessed. It would be more to do with whether the river was in the mood to let me go. I had no intention of paddling it and instead looked for a way of portaging around (see photo 20, plate section).

The next morning I launched my canoe a little upstream of the waterfall. I needed to be careful to get off the water in good time and not be drawn into it accidentally. My landing spot was well marked from my reconnaissance and I made a safe landfall. Imagining paddling the waterfall made the portage with its steep rocky outcrops and dense undergrowth all the more pleasant. If I were in a hurry then it would have seemed hard work.

When it was safe to do so I launched the canoe just below the waterfall. Given the low water levels in the rivers over the previous two days I had been dreading this stretch, believing that it would be too low to paddle. Happily the dam was releasing a 'compensation flow' and, although I would have preferred the water level a little higher, there was sufficient flow to find a deep water passage all the way down. The realisation brought with it an adrenaline rush because the Upper Tummel is a favourite river for white-water enthusiasts. I would need to be on my toes and not make mistakes.

Upon launching I drifted towards a grade two to three rapid – a difficult level if you are trying to decide whether to portage or paddle. Whereas a grade two is normally easy and a grade five too dangerous, everything that lies between causes problems because of the careful decision-making required. Added to this was the fact that I did not have a helmet with me. I had chosen not to take one on the basis that I would only be paddling rapids that I felt capable of paddling, but now there was no room for error. If I did capsize I'd be vulnerable to head injury.

Rapid after rapid passed by. On each occasion the decision to paddle or portage was a good one. By 'good' I mean 'safe', as I did not capsize nor suffer any injury. Running the rapids allowed me to play around with another skill: 'snubbing', where you use your pole to slow down on a rapid. It is simply a case of planting the pole onto the riverbed in front of you and using it to decrease speed. It was particularly useful because some of the Tummel rapids were quite shallow; it was difficult to get the paddle deep enough in the water to effectively back paddle and slow down. It was also useful for rocky rapids as the leverage you can get from prising off the riverbed can quickly alter the canoe's direction. Slowing the canoe down provides more time to think your line through and get out if things start to go wrong. I was able to do just that when I came round a corner to see two fang-like boulders just under the water obstructing my passage. It is not the easiest thing in the world to slow down a fully laden canoe in white water and then jump clear while not letting the canoe escape down-river on its own – but it can be fun: at least, it was on this occasion.

I used a handy trick to help me decide whether to portage or paddle a rapid. If, when standing up, I could see the whole rapid to where it became flat then, if there were no apparent obstacles, I paddled it. If I couldn't see the exit but could at least see an eddy I could make then I would also paddle. I had to be sure though, particularly in the very long ones, to check the whole length for any sign of camouflaged drops or trees that might have entangled me.

Sometimes not everything went quite to plan. On one grade two to three rapid a midstream rock I had not seen spun me round and I found myself speeding downstream facing the wrong way. I then realised that I had not fully scouted the exit, which was narrow and tricky. With my heart in my mouth and as much aplomb as I could muster, I applied what skill I could to reverse slalom through large midstream boulders and over a ledge into a pool of flat water – a successful outcome that resulted more from good fortune than skill.

My next adventure wasn't long in coming. On the approach to the next rapid the water set to the left of the river and disappeared over a lip. The water was being channelled over a series of rocky ledges and from above the rapid I could not see the end of it. With no idea of what to expect at the start, middle or end I got out to inspect.

The rapid was in fact a long chute. Looking at the photo I took of it (see photo 21, plate section), I am reminded of the adrenaline that was coursing through my veins at the time. The rapid was certainly navigable. Since it contained no bends I would not have to manoeuvre the canoe, just keep it running in a straight line. I figured I could do it but not without swamping. It was the consequence of swamping that bothered me. If there were any submerged rocks that caused the canoe to broach, the force of its laden weight would crumple it around the obstacle and perhaps me too. It was the only rapid I looked at and thought, 'I'd like to paddle that', but didn't. It will be there another day if I decide to return with an unladen canoe and much more buoyancy than I had then.

The final rapid of the Upper Tummel was a sustained grade two to three boulder-strewn stretch that set first against one side of the river, then the other, then back again. Checking, setting, reverse ferry gliding, breaking in and out of the current, I was continually shifting my weight around the canoe to adjust the trim. The canoe was constantly being moved through points of balance that required sometimes major but more often tiny adjustments. I was not just paddling a canoe, I was caught up in a kinaesthetic flow that required the utmost concentration. The results were absorbing and exciting. Who needs high performance cars for excitement?

At the end of this river stretch I was pleased to note that I had managed to canoe the whole of the Upper Tummel without swamping. Filled with a sense of well-being I looked ahead to see that Loch Tummel opened up before me. The loch was flat calm. I reached for my otter-tail with the knowledge that after a few leisurely strokes my mind would drift into some recess where thoughts would begin to stir. Just as metals are forged in a crucible, thoughts too emerge from a place where they first simmer and then burn brightly as the flames are fanned.

The dream that emerged was a recurring one about how the transition from living a consumer-led industrial lifestyle to something more sustainable might come about, again starting with the ontological statement that humanity is inseparable from nature. The Norwegian philosopher Arne Naess developed his own thinking around that, calling it an 'ecological ontology'. David Suzuki added to this when he said 'we are not just connected to nature – we are nature'.

> You and I don't end at our fingertips or skin – we are connected through air, water and soil; we are animated by the same energy from the same source in the sky above. We *are* quite literally air, water, soil, energy and other living creatures.

It is often difficult to see how this vision of who we are translates into everyday life, largely because the connections are often hidden. This is certainly the case for experiences in the outdoors. Climbing a mountain does not in itself lead to people thinking or acting sustainably. Similarly the act of canoeing around my home does not in itself suggest that I am doing so because I don't want to fly to exotic locations for an adventure. The relationship between adventure and our wider social and environmental obligations is not always clear. In this sense solutions to sustainable living are not inherent in the everyday activities we choose to pursue. Bert Horwood sums this up when he says that experiences such as I am describing are morally flexible as they have 'no clear intrinsic moral value'.

If someone's primary purpose when canoeing is to have an adventurous experience it would appear that whatever intrinsic moral value can be said to exist is restricted to the satisfaction of self. In this sense canoeing is an act of consumerism. However, if people are motivated by an ecological ontology then they would seek to find everyday satisfaction within an expanded sense of self that includes nature. What we have here are two very different motivating stimuli. In the first example there is the desire to spend time outdoors to satisfy self and in the second there is the desire to spend more time outdoors specifically to explore and purposefully seek out a sustainable lifestyle. The good news is that the two need not be incompatible. As Bert Horwood points out, together they represent 'a more powerful way to influence the transformation of the world towards some set of comprehensive, biospherically benign principles'.

This is the emergence of the source of truth I have been seeking since I sat in lectures rooms listening to Barry, Nev and Pete. Experiences in the outdoors, with all their emotional and cognitive complexity, have the potential to transform the theoretical principles of an ecological ontology into something that can be brought into the everyday lives of individuals.

For this to happen one of the first notions that has to be challenged is the cult of the individual. It is the celebration of the individual that, at the expense of wider society and nature, feeds consumerist lifestyles. There needs to be a clear understanding of the difference between the development of self-esteem and self-awareness. Self-esteem is promoted when one feels good about oneself. We canoe, we hillwalk, we buy consumer products all to make us feel good. However, the same can be said of people who take drugs, steal cars to go joy-riding, or travel to exotic places. The pursuit of self-esteem is about the gratification of self where the presence of moral values is not clear.

This preoccupation with the self changes when the individual comes to see their actions in relation to the wider self that is self-awareness. The self-aware person modifies their actions in relation to other people around them and within the governing limits of what the planet can endure. When looking into a mirror, a person hoping to develop their self-esteem will see themselves. A person hoping to develop their self-awareness will see reflected back the planet and with it an understanding of the dependence of humanity on nature.

So, to follow Thoreau's advice, the things we do and don't do in life need to be guided by a clear moral framework of shared values. There is no need to search for a magical solution because the answers are all around us if we care to look. We know, for example, that all life is organised along the same patterns and principles. It is only since the industrial epoch that humanity has slipped outside of these patterns and principles. We do not need to invent sustainable communities – examples already exist. Capra says, 'A sustainable human community is one designed in such a manner that its ways of life, businesses, economy, physical structures and technologies do not interfere with nature's inherent ability to sustain life'.

There is no suggestion here that living such a lifestyle will be easy. It takes a lot of hard work to research whether your purchases are 'environmentally friendly' or 'fairly traded'. However, this information is becoming increasingly available. What is required first and foremost is will-power. This strength of character is necessary to adopt an ecological ontology and use it as a platform for decision-making to guide the production, distribution and consumption of goods and services.

There was barely a ripple on the surface of Loch Tummel and hardly a breath of wind. So when the osprey crashed into the water behind me, the noise was startling. Its scientific name is *Pandion haliaetus* although it is known colloquially as a fish eagle or fish hawk. It also has a Gaelic name, lasgair, which means 'fisherman'. As its various names suggest its diet is almost exclusively fish. It is a bird supremely adapted to its environment. Its long wingspan (5–6 feet) is more than a little useful in its long migration from Africa. Its outer toe is reversible so that once it catches a fish it can line it up like a torpedo so that it is more aerodynamic in flight. I looked around to see predator and prey. The moment they met changed the future of each. One was experiencing a deadly embrace while the other set to live another day – interconnectednes. With a vigorous flutter of its wings to shake water from its feathers the osprey flew away to a roosting perch to feed.

The warm, calm day made me happy just to be. I was content to recline and let the odd gentle gust of wind move me further down the loch. Soaking in the views I noticed that the Loch Tummel hills were not as steep as they were around Loch Rannoch. These hills are wooded and support agriculture – there is a lived-in look to the landscape, with crofts and cottages dotted around. The afternoon passed in this fashion and by evening the loch narrowed and the dam at its east end appeared.

It turned out to be a tricky portage, involving lowering the canoe and equipment from the top of the dam down a steep slope to the river below. To do it safely I looped a sling around a sturdy tree and clipped both ends with a karibiner. The rope was then threaded through the karibiner using a friction hitch ready to lower. I was tempted to stay the night deep in the gorge below, but the clock was ticking. I had arranged to meet a television crew in a few days to be interviewed about my journey. The date had been arranged some time ago and it was the only part of the journey where I had to be in a specific place at a given time. So I paddled on down the Lower Tummel, which proved to be one of the most enjoyable paddling days of the whole journey, requiring great concentration and technical paddling to negotiate the many tight grade three turns.

With darkness falling I approached the very last rapid on the river – the Linn of Tummel. The Linn consists of two drops, one after the other. There was no chance of paddling it safely so, with the roar of the fall in my ears, I inched as close as possible in order to reduce the length of portage. Everything was going well until my paddle blade became trapped in a rocky ledge. With the paddle firmly wedged the current caught the canoe and began to draw it into the main stream. I ended up facing back up-river with the stern of my canoe aiming right into the heart of the fall. As the canoe moved further into the current the paddle started to bend to the point where I had to either let it go or let it snap. If I let go I would have a matter of seconds to grab my spare and then paddle forcefully upstream away from the fall. In the split second I had to work things through I knew I could do it. The challenge was to control my nerves.

With as much confidence as I could muster I let go of the paddle (which catapulted towards the river bank) and reached for the otter-tail wedged under the front seat. Thankfully it freed easily and, just as I knew I could, but feared I wouldn't, I paddled hard upstream and back into the safety of an eddy.

Still my problems were not over. It had not occurred to me that portaging would be a problem. The right-hand side of the bank consisted of steep rocky ledges that were wet and very slippery. To portage there required negotiating a fifty-metre stretch with some technical difficulty. I rigged up a safety rope as a handrail to prevent me from slipping into the water and a pulley system to pendulum the canoe across. As darkness had well and truly fallen I ended up having to do it by torchlight. However, even this moment was not without its magic. Delicate necklaces of toad spawn adorned the shallow pools I had to pass.

Completely exhausted by the exercise and in a post-adrenaline stupor I was more than relieved to be setting up my tent by the side of Loch Faskally. Imagine my surprise in the morning when I had another look at the fall. Running from the top of the Linn to the bottom was a channel with a flow of water running through it. Had I known of its existence I would have been inside my sleeping bag long before dark.

11

The connected self

Loch Faskally at dawn is a beautiful place to be. The rivers Garry and Tummel meet there between steeply wooded hills. Two male mallards with their distinctive green heads and long broad bills kept a wary eye on me as I launched my canoe. I followed them for a little while, seeking their tolerance and companionship. When I got too close their legs paddled faster and a bow wave rose up in front of their chests as they sought to keep a certain distance between them and me. They had business to attend to. There was food to find, females to fight over and predators to avoid. Feeling that they probably saw me as a predator I left them in peace to get on with their lives.

Ahead I saw the dam at the end of Loch Faskally. My map showed a road and path along its south-western shore which I had expected would make for an easy portage. In reality the footpath was narrow and full of people out for early morning dog walks. I had to fight my way against the throng of people to arrive at the dam. It's strange because the throng was only three, but after getting used seeing so few of my fellow carbon-based beings, three seemed like a crowd.

By the time I got to the dam it was busy with tourists viewing the salmon ladder, a popular visitor attraction. My trolley was useless for the portage and I ended up threading my way through a complicated walkway of railings and switchback concrete stairways against a growing throng of bewildered faces. They had come to watch salmon pursuing their destiny, not some strange life-form with an artificial carapace trying to understand his.

It seemed that the salmon were not swimming up the fish ladder, as all attention was focused on my efforts. A salmon's passage upstream through the ladder is easy compared to what I was doing. I like to think it was awe that I saw on the faces of those who watched as I manhandled the canoe over, under and through what seemed to me an assault course. I'm pretty sure, though, that most folks were wondering at the levels of stupidity people were capable of. After all, was a canoe not supposed to be on the water instead of being pirouetted above head height through busy visitor attractions? (See photo 22, plate section.)

A complicated series of stairways full of people led down to the road where at last I'd be able to put the canoe onto the trolley. I could have asked everyone to stay off the stairs and allow me to pass but lowering the canoe around twenty feet to a carpark seemed a better option. The lower looked straightforward except for the shiny Mercedes Benz sitting right below.

Always keen to accept a challenge I began setting up the sling, karibiner and rope. As I lowered the canoe it ended up precariously near the bonnet of the Mercedes. I tied it off to go below and have a better look. Taking my camera with me I wanted a photograph of the canoe pointed rocket-like at this icon of conspicuous consumption. Just then the owner appeared and noticed the canoe dangling above the car bonnet and me with camera poised. The driver and car scurried off, leaving me to ruminate. In that moment where the internal combustion engine retreated from the threat of the canoe it seemed to me, at least metaphorically, that David had just defeated Goliath. The epitome of growth economics and modern travel had retreated when confronted by a simple craft of ancient heritage.

After so many bumps and scrapes on the shallow rivers up the mountains it felt good to be launching below the dam on the greater volume rivers of the lower watershed. Soon the River Tummel joined the River Tay and I was close to smelling the sea air again. After two weeks of forcing my way up rivers and over moors and mountains it was a sublime feeling to be on a conveyor belt taking me in the direction I wanted to go. The sixty kilometres of river had lots of grade two white water, presenting a natural rollercoaster that would gently usher me all the way to the sea.

With thirty-five kilometres under my belt and daylight fading I spied an island as a possible camp spot. No sooner had I begun to slow down for a better look than I was hailed from the bank: 'no camping on the island please!' I had passed this way some years before and had heard the same voice say the same thing. Changes have come about since I first heard the voice. In 2003 the Scottish parliament enacted land reform legislation that provided statutory access for everyone. So long as access is conducted 'responsibly' then I had a legal right to camp. It was odd because although I heard the voice I could not see its owner, who was camouflaged by the trees lining the riverbank. The disembodied voice emphasised that what I heard was in fact a voice from the past, from a time when a landowner felt that the title deeds they held provided an exclusive right to the land. Despite the fact that the island looked an ideal location I was not in the mood for a fight. I needed a restful night before meeting the camera crew. Further downstream a stand of trees provided a more welcoming place to camp.

I woke the next morning with several kilometres to travel to meet the film crew. It was early and still dark when I launched my canoe as I was keen not to be late for the appointment. The early morning mist clung to the land and a warm day looked in prospect as the rising sun burned it off. For the time being, though, it was cold, and my fingers were numb as I tried to massage some circulation into them. It was with some relief that I rounded a corner and saw a fishing hut with a figure standing outside. The figure was gesticulating to me, mimicking the movement of a cup to the mouth. With a sense of *deja vu* I remembered meeting him once before.

As I drew closer the friendly face of Dennis Buchan came into view. Dennis is the ghillie for the Kercock beat. Over tea I reminded him that he had asked me in for tea once before and we shared stories. Well, the idea that we shared stories was not quite true, because although Dennis was interested in what I was doing he is a gifted story-teller, the likes of whom I feel compelled to listen to.

Dennis told me about the sea lampreys he had seen spawning in the river. Five females and one male had worked as a team, digging trenches in which to lay then fertilise the eggs. He had watched as each lamprey placed its sucker onto a stone, lifted it and moved it aside, excavating upstream as they went. When one lamprey on its own could not find the strength to move a large stone another would notice the struggle and come alongside to help. The lampreys excavated a trench six feet wide, twenty-two feet long and six inches deep. There they laid their bright white eggs. Remarkably, they dug, spawned and filled in the trench as they went. Until then lampreys had only ever been observed spawning in pairs. Dennis thought it might be the first time a group had been observed spawning together.

It all seemed quite astonishing so he alerted scientists at the nearby freshwater fisheries laboratory by Loch Faskally. Unfortunately their sea lamprey specialist was not available but they did despatch two other scientists who witnessed the lampreys working in pairs to move the larger stones. The lamprey specialist arrived three days later and was able to gather field data on the trench.

Dennis also spoke of the dog otter that frequented the riverbank and the ospreys that regularly fished that stretch of river. He talked about them with a great sense of pride and I commented that people in his profession could see otters and ospreys as a threat to the salmon and his livelihood. Dennis's reply was direct and profound. He believed that part of his job was to educate others about the wider ecology of the river and not just focus on the catching of salmon. He shared this ethos with his clients, so when the dog otter or osprey appeared they would down rods to watch the iconic species hunting the same prey as themselves. In many ways this could be counted as interconnected thinking and I listened to Dennis for over an hour before taking my leave. Dennis is an educator in the truest sense of the word. He brings the stories of the landscape to life with his detailed knowledge. Before schools and universities invented subjects and gave them names, people like Dennis were telling the stores of life unencumbered by fancy titles.

I arrived early for my appointment with the film crew. Meg and Mark from Triple Echo Productions were to film and interview me about the journey for a programme called *The Adventure Show*. I remembered my apprehension when I first met Meg and Mark to explain my journey. My fear was that they would be interested only in the adventure aspect and not the reason for doing it. My fears were completely unfounded as they transformed my own loose thoughts into televised material. I know that not everyone can or wants to do this sort of journey, so it was important that I could communicate not just with active outdoors people but also with armchair activists and vicarious participants about the powerful motivations for people considering lifestyle changes. We spent four hours together and produced a four-minute clip which reached a wide audience.

After bidding farewell to Meg and Mark I continued down what is a familiar stretch for most white-water canoeists between Stanley and Thistlebrig. As a fledgling kayaker I cut my teeth there. It may be only two kilometres in length but it is probably one of the best-loved sections of white water in the UK.

It is a favoured stretch for anglers too. Some people make much of the rivalry between fishermen and canoeists, which is understandable given the popularity of both activities. But the rivalry is often misplaced. I remember on one occasion kayaking through the Stanley to Thistlebrig stretch and arriving at the final rapid to find a group of kayakers performing stunts. They had brought with them a portable stereo that was turned up full volume. I have also encountered abuse from anglers for no apparent reason other than my presence. However, these are isolated incidents. Canoeists and kayakers who seek out peace and solitude for their recreation have a lot in common with anglers who will stand for hours in one spot, or slowly move down a river soaking up the ambience of nature's sights, sounds and smells. It is too easy to shoehorn people into polar opposites. When we forget about activities and focus instead on experiences we very often come up with a different picture.

With the river moving me along quickly I arrived at Luncarty to meet Jane for the only night on the journey where I would be insulated from the outdoors. We treated ourselves to bed, breakfast and dinner out. Apart from the niceties, the logistical purpose was to exchange my canoe for a sea kayak. I had anticipated that repacking my equipment, which fitted easily in the three large bags in my canoe, into the two small hatches in my sea kayak would take some time. I'd planned to do most of the repacking under a roof in case of rain. In the end we had a sunny day which made the transfer easy and we completed the job quickly, which meant I had more time to spend with Jane.

When I set off with my sea kayak from Luncarty my first feeling was of claustrophobia. I couldn't move around, stand up or get an elevated view down rapids. I was encased within a lump of plastic that was supposed to keep me safe in the exposed waters of the North Sea. Thankfully it was not long before a degree of familiarity returned. The two-bladed kayak paddle helped me to move through the water much more quickly than my single-bladed canoe paddle was able to do. The hydrodynamic design of the sea kayak helped too, because of its longer, sleeker lines.

Meeting the film crew and changing craft disrupted the routine of my journey. It wasn't unpleasant, but certainly by the time I got underway I was happy that all the logistics were behind me. However, as the day wore on I sensed the growing presence of the sea and began to feel nervous. More than ever I thought of not having trained through the winter to build up my physical condition. Even more worrying was that I had never been exposed to the sorts of seas I could expect, nor practiced my canoe roll for two or three years. On top of that there were the injuries to my wrists, shoulder and back. I began thinking of myself as an accident waiting to happen.

It is common to think of evolution as a process whereby single-celled life evolved into multi-cellular life; somewhere in the distant past humans emerged with their superior intellect and outstripped other multi-cellular organisms to sit proudly at the pinnacle of evolution above all other forms of life. This creation myth of dominance and superiority over nature is so deeply ingrained in our culture that we rarely pause to question it. However, with the prospect of humanity facing a crisis of survival at some time in the not too distant future, there is good reason to pause and question.

In some ways it is understandable that a species which evolved in such amazing ways and developed the capacity for analytical thought should come to think of itself as a superior life-form. After all, chimpanzees don't build aeroplanes, mycetopholids don't drive cars, and worms do not fly rockets to the moon (not yet at least). When viewed through the spectacles of human achievement there is no doubt that evolution has endowed our own species with something spectacular. However, environmental philosophers have a name for this way of viewing the world, which they call 'anthropocentrism', a paradigm based on human-centeredness where nature is subordinated to human need.

Those who suggest that the anthropocentric paradigm is the central problem of the ecological crisis would offer an ecocentric paradigm as an alternative. Arne Naess's ecological ontology is one example. Such a paradigm would celebrate co-operation and not competition with nature. It would require a shift from dominating nature to finding equality within it, from reductionism to holism, from shallow ecology to deep ecology, and from hierarchy to understanding humanity within the web of life. Well, that may be the theory, but for me there still seems something missing.

I first met Jim Cheney at an environmental education conference in Whitehorse, Canada and afterwards six of us spent three weeks canoeing the Wind and Peel rivers in the Northern Yukon. I spent a long time talking with Jim about environmental philosophy. I learned a lot from him and others on the trip, some of whom were leading lights in environmental philosophy. It wasn't just the conversation, though. Jim has a presence that is both learned and gentle, underpinned with a great sense of mischief.

Four years later Jim came to visit Scotland and we set off down the River Spey in a canoe to renew our friendship and revisit old conversations. Later in the day we stopped for lunch and sat chatting on the riverbank. Two ladies walked past and Jim and I both said, 'Hello.' One of the ladies said, 'You two look deep in thought.' I said something like we were trying to save the world. One of the ladies replied, 'You are too late, we've done that already.' All four of us laughed heartily as the two ladies continued on their way.

I only saw the humour in the meeting but Jim read something in it that was not at first apparent to me. In previous conversations Jim had told me he had grown tired of academic discourse. The theoretical discussions dominant in environmental philosophy had become so academic he worried that it had become more important to talk about the human-nature relationship than experience it. Consequently nature became abstracted and fought over by those defending different paradigms. Weary of such discourse and looking beyond the abstract, the important thing for Jim was how to 'be' in the world. Jim helped me to see that there is a difference between being in the world and theorising about being in the world. There on the riverbank Jim and I were theorising about the world when two ladies walked by who were 'in' the world.

It may seem overly presumptions to assume too much from this one encounter. It does raise interesting questions about paradigms, though, particularly the discussion between anthropocentrism and ecocentrism. Does it really matter whether people operate from an anthropocentric or ecocentric viewpoint? For me this is where the problem lies. It is not so much the theoretical differences that prevent people from acting sustainably. It is more to do with the lack of starting points. Ecocentrism offers a vision of the sorts of values central to a sustainable society but it offers little guidance on how to begin from the start point of people's everyday lives. There is a real danger that ecocentricsm as a vision will fall into the very trap that it is trying to avoid, simply because it is conceived by people. In other words ecocentrism is an anthropocentric conception (at least at a theoretical level).

It might appear that I have now argued myself into a stalemate. On the one hand I am saying that ecocentrism is too theoretical as a vision and on the other that there are few starting points for sustainable lifestyles. However this is only the case if the argument is based on 'either, or'. Why not use the vision of ecocentrism as something that offers direction? It is relatively easy to theorise and envision a sustainable future – a general direction. If the start point is not the vision but the everyday experiences that people have of life then the endless cycle of theoretical argument can be broken. However, the vision must be translated into something that is relevant to people everywhere, otherwise it remains an ideal. You don't teach or preach reality, you live it by practising it. The difficult part is mobilising the effort in the first place. What is required is a movement from thinking about an ecocentric society to developing momentum for us as a species to *want* to live sustainably. There is a real need to work with the stories of everyday people in their everyday lives.

The River Tay widens as it reaches Perth. A cormorant appeared in an obvious state of distress. It had a fish hook in its mouth with a float attached. It was dragging the float around the surface. I resolved to catch it and in anticipation located my fixed-blade knife to cut the line. In the back of my mind I realised I might have to use it for another purpose because in its condition the bird would never be able to catch fish and would most likely die from starvation. However, it still had a lot of energy left and dived below the surface every time I got near. The chase began to cause me distress because I knew that the pressure of diving would not only make the hook bite deeper but inflict even more pain. In the end I knew that there was no chance of me catching the bird so I left it to its fate.

As I paddled on I was left with a great sense of sadness, even though I knew that around the world there would be plenty of other cormorants suffering as this one had. But knowing that did not affect me anywhere near as much as the personal encounter. I knew also that the distress I felt for the cormorant would fade as the days went by.

From this I concluded two things. The first is that for humans to better understand their interconnection with nature they need to have direct encounters. The second is that because the power of the experience wanes over time, encounters of this type need to be repeated and part of everyday lifestyles. This is why *direct* experiences outdoors are central to understanding the human-nature relationship. It is understanding this relationship in its theoretical and experiential complexity that leads towards 'the connected self'. I guess it is also what Jim meant when he said we need to 'be' in the world and not just think about it. Does it matter to the cormorant if I look at its situation from an anthropocentric or ecocentric viewpoint?

The urban sprawl of Perth gave way to an agricultural landscape and the river opened out into a shallow estuary lined with sandbanks. They have fairly evocative names such as 'The Hard', 'McInnes' Bank', 'Durward's Scalp' and 'Sure as Death Bank'. I wondered if McInnes and Durward were captains of ships that foundered there. Their names reminded me that the North Sea was right around the corner.

After a night's sleep I set off with the wind and tide in my favour, my mood matching the shining sun. I crossed the Firth at the point where the Admiralty Chart warned of turbulence but I found none. Over my left shoulder Dundee began to fade into the distance.

In the nineteenth century Dundee was Europe's jute capital. The United Kingdom's main whaling fleet was based there too. Using Dundee as its main port the fleet went first to the Arctic. When that was fished out the fleet headed south to the Antarctic. Dundee was an obvious hub because it catered for a variety of industries. One of the uses of whale oil was to soften jute fibres prior to weaving. The whales were also sought for their blubber which when refined was used as oil for street lamps and the

Map 4 – The coastal passage

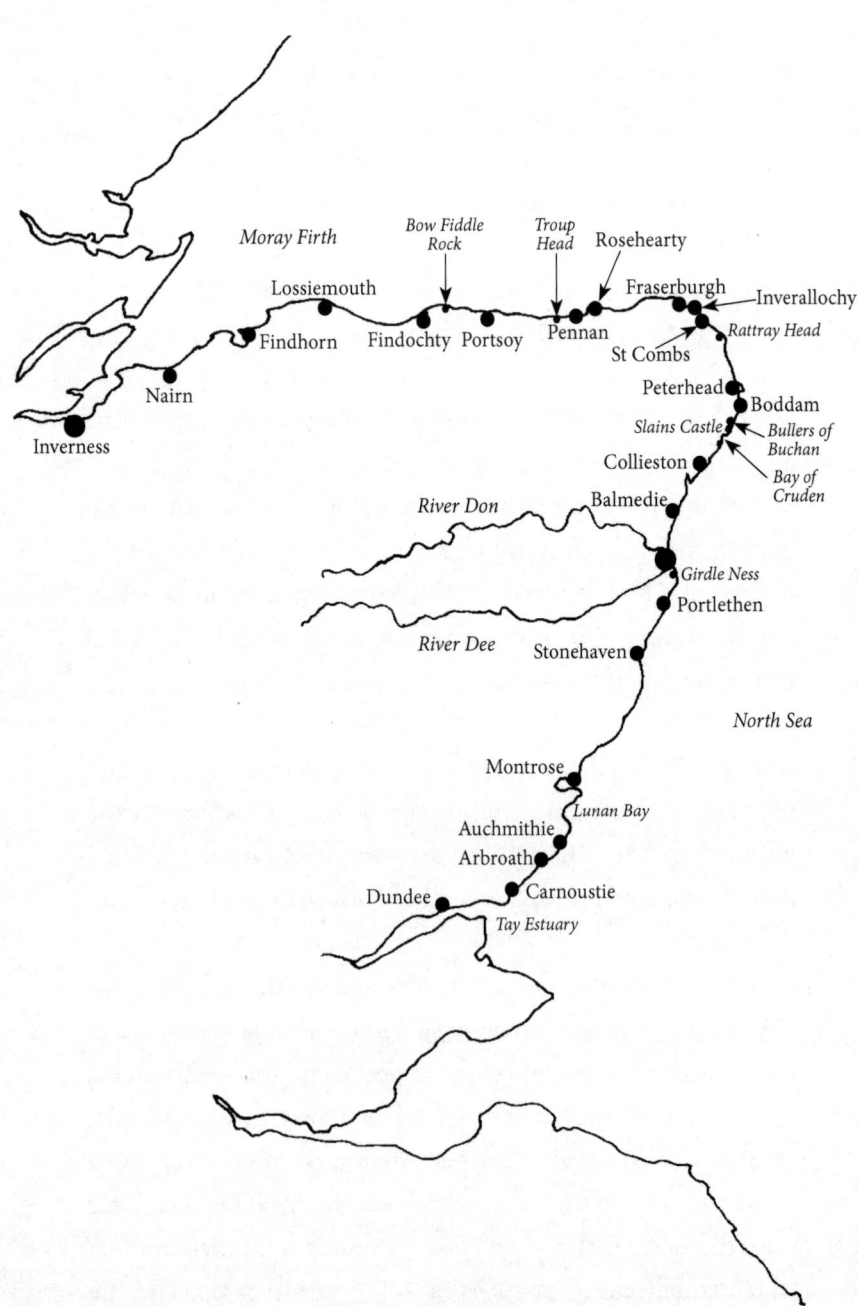

200

making of candles. Whales brought light in the night to cities that would otherwise have been dark. Ironically this light allowed people to work longer days, making them more productive. This contributed to expanding the economy, with the result that more workers were required to keep up with demand, leading to the need for more whale blubber to light up more people's evenings. The relentless pursuit of growth meant only one thing for the whales and it wasn't long before the Antarctic, like the Arctic, became over-fished. The lights went out on the whaling industry in the late nineteenth century.

At the turn of the century explorers followed the whalers' route to the north and south poles from Dundee. Having the ship-building expertise to design craft that could withstand the icy conditions found at the poles, Dundee was a natural choice as the centre for polar exploration. Indeed Dundee led the world in the building of ships designed for polar work. The royal research ship *Discovery* was built there and her captain, Robert Falcon Scott, set sail from there on one of his first expeditions to Antarctica, which was to culminate in his ill-fated race to reach the South Pole before Roald Amundsen.

Approaching the sea I had to pay attention to the tides. A two-knot spring tide runs up and down the east coast which could, if I timed it right, help me on my way or could, if I didn't, slow me down. I had my VHF radio switched on, not just so that I could listen for the Coastguard's weather reports but also as a front line safety item were I to capsize. Even the way I recorded my notes changed. When I used the voice recorder in the canoe I could relax and take my time. In the sea kayak where the sea was restless I needed one hand on my paddle just in case the odd wave were to catch me unprepared.

At first the waves within the shelter of the Firth of Tay were small and manageable. Slowly, though, and almost imperceptibly, the nature of the waves began to change. The small waves within the Firth were created by the wind I felt on my face. It was a local wind, gentle and benign. Swell is something quite different. Swell waves are created by winds and storms a long distance from where they make landfall. The swell I was beginning to experience had its origins way out in the North Sea, perhaps some three or four hundred miles away. Those particular swell waves would have travelled together in long parallel lines to reach Scotland's east coast. There they meet shelving beaches, which cause them to accelerate and rear up into large curling waves and finally break, discharging their pent-up energy. Because of this it is quite possible to have a windless day yet still have large swell waves. I was soon to be reminded of this at my cost. To begin with, though, I had nothing to worry about. Leaving the shelter of the Firth of Tay and rounding the point at Buddon Ness there was little wind, the sea was kind to me, and a gentle swell allowed me the time I needed to rediscover my 'sea legs'.

Further on and as I was looking for somewhere to stop for a rest some seals waddled into the water, leaving behind a pup on the beach. Small waders were everywhere scurrying around looking for insects. Curious about the abandoned seal pup I landed some distance away and looked out my camera. As I crept closer it became clear that it was not normal behaviour. There were many pups that size, all of which had escaped into the water with their mothers; I could see them all, heads above the water, watching my every move. Giving the pup on the sand a wide berth I approached it from the other side and could immediately see the problem. Some defect at birth, or injury thereafter, had left it blind in one eye. It looked well fed for the moment but I wondered what the future held for it as it weaned and had to become more dependent on its own hunting prowess (see photo 23, plate section).

Seeing new life in this way I sympathised with the hand that nature had dealt it. I felt as though I should have done something to help, but I didn't. I was content to leave it to whatever fate had in store. It was a very different feeling from the clear distress I felt for the cormorant. Although both were likely to starve to death in due course, I did not see the hand of my own species in the fate of the seal. Nature finds its own way of dealing with life and death, but it is the weight of the hand of my own kind to interfere with that balance that is most concerning. The cormorant was symbolic of that concern.

Wildlife was everywhere. Seals, eiders, small waders, curlews. A pair of shelducks appeared before my attention was drawn to the starkly contrasting white plumage and jet black wingtips of a gannet. The noise and presence of the sea was everywhere, restless with its movements and sounds. My whole being felt infiltrated by its presence, reminding me that my own body is largely made up of water and salt.

At Whiting Ness there are sharply contrasting geological features. There are numerous faults and bedding planes and even the old red sandstone has its own variations. Some of the rock is made up of fine-grained sandstone sediment and some of a much larger conglomerate sediment. The sea has eaten away at the 'softer' sandstone and sculpted it into wonderful shapes, leaving the coastline littered with caves and stacks. All along the coast there are stories written into the landscape that I can only wonder at. Clearly great forces are at work to create such a convoluted land mass (see photo 24, plate section).

To find some respite from the gathering wind I sneaked into the deep recess known as 'Dickmont's Den'. I say 'sneak' because my inclination had been to pass by it as the clapotis was tricky, but curiosity had the better of me. The waves were funnelling through the narrow entrance and as I paddled closer I was waiting for the rogue wave that would pick me up and surf me into the rocks. However, I passed through the funnel with no drama. Towards the back of the den I found absolute tranquillity as I was sheltered from the wind and waves. Having experienced this once I could not make myself pass the cave at The Deil's Heid without closer inspection. The coastline there is full of the history of landscape formation. I could not quench my thirst for it and promised myself I would come back.

With my senses straining at the leash I found myself scanning the coastline for the next natural wonder. It wasn't long in coming as, peering into a recessed bay, I saw something large lying high up on the beach. Drawing closer I could see it was the carcass of a whale. Approaching a dead whale from downwind is not a clever thing to do. The stench was appalling; something I can only describe as sweet, sickly and forever memorable. I paced out its length and estimated it to be twelve metres. Not being able to identify it I took a photograph that I later sent to the Hebridean Whale and Dolphin Trust. They told me that its very long flippers helped to confirm that it was a humpback whale. Not only were they able to identify it but they knew what had happened to it. They explained that humpbacks were not that common in the North Sea. This one was first reported dead the month before I came across it. When it was first examined it showed signs of having been entangled in lines, probably creel lines, which appear to have been the cause of death (see photo 25, plate section).

Looking round the carcass I could see that it had been vandalised and mutilated. The rusty leg of an old chair was protruding from its eye socket and another from its anal passage.

I felt anger at the perpetrators and a great degree of sadness for the once magnificent creature lying debased in death. Yet the anger seems illogical and a little strange. Illogical because at one level it was only a piece of rotting flesh. Although I saw it as mutilated and vandalised I could easily think the same when slaughterhouse animals are electrocuted or have a 'captive bolt', known euphemistically as a 'humane killer', fired into their brains. But it is not death, nor the manner it came about, nor even what happened to the carcass afterwards that troubled me. I know deep down that I was playing a clever mind game with myself. It was easy for me to look at the whale and find some theoretical explanation about what was wrong and look for other people to blame.

But by doing that I would be looking in the wrong place for answers. I remember as a child using an air rifle to shoot at garden birds for fun. I guess I did not have a highly developed value system to appreciate living things. Nowadays when I recall those experiences I shudder, knowing that my actions were cruel and wanton.

I could spend a long time theorising about it and coming up with arguments that would justify my actions (as if I was only a child). Worse, perhaps, I could conveniently overlook the incident, pretend it did not happen and not think about it. One thing I can't do is to theorise away the feelings I have for what happened. This I think reveals one of the major obstacles in our search for sustainable lifestyles. Our clever minds are constantly trying to rationalise our behaviour, a natural function of our intellect. However, in rationalising our behaviour we come to blame ideas and not ourselves for our actions or inaction. Each of us can say, 'It is not my fault that the amount of carbon in the atmosphere is causing the planet to warm.' This allows us to look into a mirror and see reflected back a clear conscience. However, when the mirror is framed by an ecological ontology, the reflection is an image of responsibility and not of excuses.

As I looked at the vandalised whale I used it as a mirror to see who was to blame. The image I first saw was that of a gang of youths on a Saturday afternoon with nothing better to do. But as I looked closer the image that finally sharpened was myself. I was not just thinking about the actions of those who did it, I was feeling the hurt inside that I have caused in my own life. It may not have been me that stuck a chair leg up the whale's anus but it was someone like me.

It is the complete and utter directness of experiences such as these that are the source of me wanting to do something 'about the planet'. I am ashamed by the cruelty in my past but acknowledge how the direct experience of such things makes the relationship between people and planet more visible. I am not presenting these stories as a justification for cruelty. The point is to show how outdoor experiences have a powerful emotional rawness that is direct and compelling and can be harnessed as motivating factors towards sustainable lifestyles.

One of the reasons that experiences in the outdoors are so important lies in the growing body of enthusiasts who look towards the great outdoors for their recreation. This sector comprises individuals spanning all classes, all professions, all ages and genders. These people, through their familiarity with the outdoors, represent a link to many aspects of society where decisions are made about the production, distribution and consumption of goods and services. Those who go outdoors represent a social web not unlike the web of life itself. This is why it is so important that those who take part in outdoor activities know of the relationship between people and place because once motivated they are in a position to do something about it across a broad range of societal functions (for example local and central government, industry and economics and so on).

The heightened sense of grief brought on by the whale encounter also brought into sharp focus some other personal issues. I had been thinking a lot about my own mortality as the sea state became rougher, a feeling that was making me yearn for home and normality. Seeing what had been done to the whale was a chastening experience and I moved on from that place a little sadder but, I hoped too, a little more humble.

Further on I encountered my first razorbills and puffins. I pulled abreast of Auchmithie, a place I had wanted to visit since reading about it in Brian Wilson's book *Blazing Paddles*, in which he describes circumnavigating the coastline of Scotland in a kayak. It was still early in the day and I had to resist the temptation to continue. Until then I had been happy not to rush and had been content with making progress as conditions allowed. For the first time, though, I felt a strong temptation to speed up and the idea of a schedule and making an end to the journey kept entering my head. In terms of distance travelled I was much nearer the end than the beginning, and the end was beginning to play a greater part in my thinking. The end became a target.

Resisting the urge to continue I went exploring and found the cave in the red sandstone where Brian Wilson spent a night. I took comfort knowing that Brian prevailed during his own endeavours and reminded myself that in terms of dangerousness my own journey paled into considerable insignificance by comparison. Even the effort of hauling a kayak and equipment up and down beaches was much easier for me. Because Brian had a glass fibre kayak he had to protect its fragile skin by moving it up and down rocky beaches on an inflatable fender. My plastic kayak is much more forgiving. When I arrive at a beach I empty all the gear and carry it to my chosen camp spot then drag the empty kayak up the beach. On sand and softer stone I can lift the back of the kayak and push it. I also use seaweed to cushion the kayak wherever possible and on very rough parts I look for a piece of driftwood to use as a roller.

A young Czech couple had arrived on foot and occupied Brian's cave. I had anticipated spending the night there myself imagining the conversations we might have had because he too wrote about environmental awareness as part of his journey. An idea had been growing in my own mind throughout the day and as I neared Auchmithie I had been looking forward to sitting in the cave, saying it out loud and imagining Brian's response. With the Czech couple clearly settled for the night I set up my tent and had to make do with my voice recorder as a companion and recorded some vague ideas around the notion that whilst theory is important in order to explain what is wrong with the world if you want to change it you must also look inwards. In other words changing the world is an inside job. I think two sea kayakers sitting in a sea cave around a campfire would have had a lot to say about this. I still wonder how Brian would have responded had he been there.

12

An adventure too far?

I SET OFF FROM THE CAVE AT ABOUT 8 A.M. THE WIND WAS coming from the north and soon I was shivering. The morning forecast had said there would be snow on the Cairngorm Mountains and I wondered if the snow would fall in the North Sea. No matter how fast I paddled I remained cold and had to stop to run along the beach to warm up and pull on a few more layers of clothing. Soon after, I set off across Lunan Bay with the wind blowing force five from the north-west and set to increase to force six. When the wind behaves like that waves don't form into regular patterns. The changing wind direction means that the waves collide into each other, leaving the sea in a state of chaos.

Around Scurdie Ness the tide was running and I had to work hard against its flow. Straight ahead lay Montrose Basin, where the water passes through a narrow entrance and the Admiralty Pilot says the in-going and outgoing streams run at a spring rate of seven knots. Thankfully I arrived at a time when the tide was not flowing that strongly. The lighthouse provided an inviting lunch spot and relief from the strong wind. Despite the cold wind the sun was out, and sheltered from the wind the sun was warm enough to bask in. Another person had found this out too – Michelle Bates, an artist from London now living in Montrose. When I told her the purpose of my journey she said that maybe it doesn't matter if human beings are on the planet or not. That may well be the case, and it is something that James Lovelock articulates very well in his Gaia theory, but for me at least I'm not yet ready to throw in the towel and leave our survival to chance. However, a little later I did decide to throw in the towel on the day's paddling, pulling in at Johnshaven after a gruelling day of headwinds and sidewinds straining bodily sinews and testing my concentration.

When the early morning alarm clock rang it was still dark outside. I opted for a lazy start, went back to sleep and waited for the light from the rising sun to wake me. There were difficult decisions ahead because the wind was a southerly force five, meaning I could make good progress up the north coast. I was keen to make use of the wind while it was behind me but at the same time I felt pretty worn out. Even small things were proving difficult. Opening and closing hatches requires strong fingers, pushing a fist through the rubber seals of my cagoule requires strong wrists and paddling all day requires general all-round fitness. I reflected on how my lack of preparation for the journey was a bit like society's lack of preparation for the challenges of sustainability. 'Let's get fit for sustainability.' It is a thought-provoking metaphor.

After breakfast my mind was troubled and I did not feel up to the challenge of launching so went for a walk instead. I began to think that walking might be a better mode of travel than sea kayaking for this sort of contemplative journey. The sea kayaker has to be preoccupied with equipment, the weather, maintaining physical effort, concentrating on staying alive, interpreting forecasts accurately and carrying the kayak up and down beaches. With sea kayaking it is hard to paddle in a day-dream unless the conditions are calm. On this short walk my mind was alive with ideas that had been kept at bay when I was on the water.

I returned to the kayak determined to put these fears to the sword, convinced that my thoughts were some weak inner attempt to postpone the journey. The midday forecast suggested that the wind was to be south-west veering north-west force five to seven and the sea state slight to moderate. The outlook for the next day was for the wind to be from the west veering north-east force five to seven. I took this to mean a strengthening wind for the rest of the day and that at some point tomorrow it would go clockwise round to the area that I least wanted it – a headwind.

I looked to the sky for other evidence: the cloud formations suggested things were going to get worse before they got better. The distinctive lenticular clouds (shaped like flying saucers) provided a good indication that strong winds were on their way. With such changes imminent I needed to keep a careful eye on the weather. As I broke camp, folded my tent and loaded the kayak I was aware of the wind increasing and the sea building behind me. My imagination wandered. I thought of a lion patrolling a camp perimeter in the African bush and I felt like human prey. I imagined the sea, like the lion, having me for its breakfast. The key factor in the relationship was not really me. It was up to the sea, and not me, to decide what would happen next. I was acutely aware of my growing insignificance as I busied myself packing bags, hoping the predator would leave me alone.

On days when it was windy with swell and a lot of no-landing areas I try not to think of the day's paddle as a whole. Instead I think more about the next bay or the next headland in much the same way as the winter mountaineer picks their way through avalanche-prone slopes by linking 'islands of safety'. Little by little it helps to manage the process, a process involving not only my physical safety but my psychological safety too. Maybe there is a metaphor somewhere there about how we might relate to complicated environmental issues. By working out small but achievable goals we can more easily measure progress towards the larger vision. Acting locally while thinking globally.

At first the sea was manageable and I talked into my voice recorder. However, I got a flavour of what was in store when the waves passing under the kayak suddenly got larger. I had to drop the recorder onto the spraydeck and reach for a support stroke to balance myself until the big ones passed through. Forward momentum provides stability but being stationary is much more precarious. Luckily the sticky texture of the waterproof map case meant that the recorder did not slip off into the sea and I thankfully tucked it safely away in the pocket of my buoyancy aid where it remained for the rest of the day.

It was a bit like playing nip and tuck with the sea. I nipped out from the shelter of a bay or headland feeling very vulnerable, and as long as things went well my feelings were of thanks. But I didn't know who or what I was thanking. Maybe it was something to do with being religious in my youth and giving thanks through prayer to that God. Nowadays I don't believe in a God, but maybe it takes tough situations for such questions to arise. And although I don't believe there is anyone out there to thank I still wanted somebody or something to look after me. I'm not really sure what spirituality is but I do know that it is different out there than it is when I am sitting in my office. Thinking about it is different from feeling it in your bones. That is why I adopted the puffins as my guardian angels. Puffins are Jane's favourite birds. I needed something to place my trust in and not just rely on myself. I needed to feel a relationship with something else. In turn, I experienced a feeling of absolute dependence. Once again I was reminded of that important tenet in environmental philosophy stating that humanity is utterly dependent on nature for its survival.

The sea is a scary place but it can be beautiful too. It is the relationship between scary and beautiful that is interesting. It can't be beautiful or scary all the time otherwise it would just be normal; it's the contrast between states that allows us to think of it as one or the other.

The coastline passed by in a blur of fear, and during a slight lull in the wind I found myself surfing some waves and whooping with delight. The wind dropped as it moved around to the north-west and the land was shielding me from its worst effects. With the change I noted that my quality of life was inversely proportional to the strength of the wind. No sooner had I congratulated myself for this insight when I was hit by a strong gust of wind from the side. When the wind blows over the land it is affected by topography. Sometimes the land contours funnel the wind, causing it to accelerate off the lips of cliff edges and direct its energy downwards. These are called 'downdraughts' and are known to capsize unwary kayakers, even wary ones too. Beyond Catterline the cliff height increased and with it the ferocity of the downdraughts. I was torn between moving from close in, where I was sheltered from the prevailing wind but exposed to the odd downdraught, and heading further offshore, where I would be exposed to the full force of the offshore wind but away from the downdraughts.

I had never paddled this coast before and had no knowledge of the nooks and crannies that local people would know that offered shelter. So when I set off with long stretches of cliffs to pass I needed to be sure that I could get to the next area on the map that I had identified as a safe landing spot. If I miscalculated the weather and got stuck in the middle then I would have to either return (hoping the place I left was still okay to land) or continue (hoping that a safe landing spot would appear ahead).

The closeness of the land offered some sense of psychological security and so I decided to hug the coast. I could see that my decision had other consequences because I disturbed a lot of seabirds. Guillemots and razorbills appeared to spook much easier than the gulls. They were taking off and landing all around me. It appeared that their downward trajectories were guided more by gravity than flight as they plummeted from high cliff tops and hit the water with a splash that looked more like a crash than a landing. It felt as though someone had fired a guillemot cartridge through their shotgun and I was being peppered with the shot. Luckily for all concerned none hit me but I did take it as a message from Neptune to move further away and leave the birds in peace. So many birds had flown over me that I could not help thinking how lucky I was not to have been spattered with their droppings. Perhaps Neptune approved of my intentions to avoid distress and let me off without reprimand.

The shelter of Castle Haven bay provided an ideal camp spot and I felt truly thankful to be entering its welcoming enclosure free from the effects of wind and wave. Throughout history the bay has been the scene of hospitality and imprisonment in equal measure. Dunnottar Castle sits high above it, surrounded on three sides by fifty-metre cliffs. On the fourth side there is a notch between the rock on which the castle stands and the mainland, a quirk of geology hewn first by erosion and then by defenders intent on improving nature's design to make the castle impregnable. Typical of strategic sites in Scotland, the castle has been inhabited by saints and fought over by kings. The Picts lived there when St. Ninian arrived to convert them to Christianity. It was the scene of one of the many feuds between William Wallace and Edward I and later between the forces of Cromwell and Charles II. The Scottish crown jewels were hidden there from Cromwell's forces.

Mary Queen of Scots stayed as a guest, and some Covenanters stayed as prisoners and were tortured for their beliefs. The castle looms large in the first Jacobite rebellion. This fluke of geology has resulted in a rich human history etched as deeply into the landscape as any history book could ever describe. Today the modern day raiders are called tourists, all anxious to take away something of their own. With the crown jewels long gone all that is left is to take some photographs. With a few of these as booty this seaborne raider returned to his tent.

The next day was again bitterly cold, so before getting on the water I went for a run. Soon after launching, somewhere just north of Stonehaven, a small tide race was running at Garron Point and a school of dolphins frolicked around me. Watching dolphins surf the bow waves of large boats is one of nature's wonderful sights. Their performance was a combination of poise, grace, agility and power as they effortlessly whiled away their time. It was clear that the dolphins were unimpressed with the bow wave coming off the front of my kayak though as they disappeared to find a bigger wave to play on.

In such conditions my mood swings were fairly large and intense. After a spell of paddling I became so cold that I stopped for a snack. As soon as I was safely on land the sun shone again, the wind dropped, and all was well with life. However, back on the water with dark clouds gathering I could see that was about to change quickly. As the wind picked up I was battered by downdraughts, the strongest of which pushed me sideways. I had to lean precariously into the wind to avoid being capsized, then had to be ready to shift my balance back when the wind eased, otherwise the effects of gravity would send me under. Every time I rounded a small point or headland I became exposed to a combination of three effects. Clapotis came from my left, a force six wind from ahead and a two-knot tidal flow from the right. The result was a maze of confused water which was just manageable as long as I maintained concentration.

With dark clouds getting ever nearer I pulled into what I thought to be Portlethen. With such gruelling conditions I had not been concentrating on my map. This had been no aesthetic experience. As I continued the land closed in to provide shelter from the wind and waves and I looked more closely at my map. Instantly I could see that I was not in Portlethen at all. I did not have time to work out exactly where I was because the dark clouds had unleashed a ferocious hailstorm. In haste, while being peppered with painful balls of ice, I managed to land and found shelter in a smelly old portacabin. Full of old sofas, tables and empty bottles of alcohol I shuddered to think what it was normally used for. However, in that moment it was heaven for me (maybe it was heaven too for the people who met there to drink). In any case I was thankful to the regulars for my temporary stay.

With a litre of hot coffee to dispose of I settled down on one of the sofas and got my map out to work out where I was.

With a sense of elation I realised that I had come further than expected and was in Cove Bay. With that sense of elation came a little embarrassment from knowing that it was four and a half kilometres from where I'd first estimated. I reassured myself that the conditions were miserable and that in any case no-one else would ever know.

The hailstorm passed, the sun took its place and I found a grassy hollow in which to lie and doze – such is the contrast of extremes. I took time to attend to some of my sores that had been getting worse the longer the journey went on. It was time to reflect too on how this was not really the way I'd hoped the journey would turn out. I had wanted it to be much less adventurous and much more contemplative. With that realisation I was keen to get back to Inverness and for the journey to end. I had to stay focused, though, and concentrate on my safety. The only possible way to encounter the sea is on its own terms. If you forget that or underestimate the sea there is a good chance you will die. And someone did die just one month before along the stretch I would be paddling tomorrow. The lone kayaker had drowned and was washed up on Balmedie beach.

More than ever I was reminded of the potential dangers of paddling alone. I was concerned for another reason too, which had nothing to do with my own safety. Not so many paddlers venture out at this time of year and seeing a solo paddler is even less likely. I hated to think that a relative of the dead paddler may just be on Balmedie beach and see me as I was passing. I know that grief can be so painful that you can wish the impossible into existence. What sorts of thoughts, feelings and hurt might I cause if I were seen? For that reason alone I had thought of trying to find a way to get a lift beyond Balmedie and start again further north.

With my troubled thoughts unresolved I settled down for the night.

Dressing the next morning was the usual pantomime. With Velcro fastenings on so many items of clothing I frequently tied myself in knots as trouser legs stuck to cagoule arms and map cases attached themselves to sandals. In the tangle of clothes and with a cagoule pulled over my head I sometimes didn't know what limb I was putting an article of clothing on. Mostly it was fun but sometimes infuriating.

My next challenge was to get out of the inlet I had stayed in. The swell was big – very big. Just like surf waves the swell waves grow in size as they accelerate up the shelving seabed to crash onto the beach. Thankfully, there was little wind to speak of when I got beyond that critical interface between land and sea. I wanted to get the timing correct to avoid the tide race that the Admiralty Pilot said ran off Girdle Ness, and I was pleased to arrive at slack water. With no tidal flow to worry about I just had to watch out for the effects of swell waves as they passed over skerries, creating large breaking waves.

Rounding the point at Girdle Ness I found that the swell was indeed large. I could see the waves coming from far out to sea. They accelerated as they passed over the skerries then stood high, poised like a horse on its rear legs, momentarily stationary, before crashing down again, leaving the skerries awash with seething water streaming off their sides. Some skerries sit above the water line while some are submerged. Kayaking through them can be compared to negotiating a safe passage through a minefield. Explosions occurred all around with the booming and crashing of waves, all at a wind speed of less than force two. The absence of significant wind enhanced the sound of the waves and I couldn't dispel the feeling of eeriness about the conditions. I was glad to leave the rough water around the skerries behind. I did take with me another memory, though. As I was working my way through the minefield I saw my first Arctic Tern of the trip, fishing nonchalantly among the crashing skerries – an example of an organism supremely adapted to its environment (unlike me!).

Immediately afterwards I came upon a line of freighters queuing up to enter Aberdeen harbour, all appearing to be vying for position. I was never going to be a winner in the competition for space but I saw there was a pilot boat escorting them one at a time. All I needed to do was cross the harbour entrance after one freighter passed and before the next arrived. Even though the swell was large it was quite rounded and not forced into the sorts of contortions that I'd struggled through at Girdle Ness. The long, long flatness of Aberdeen's beach esplanade lay ahead and enticed me across the sea lane.

Safely on the other side I began whistling the bagpipe tune called 'The Fittie Boatman'. It is through Aberdeen harbour that the River Dee empties into the North Sea. At the harbour entrance is the old fishing village of Footdee, known locally as Fittie. The Fittie Boatman was written in honour of those men whose job it was to secure the boats tying up in the harbour. The tune name has its origins there and therefore celebrates local geography and culture. Every time the tune is played history becomes a living tradition and not simply a reflection of the past.

With nearly twenty-five kilometres of golden sandy beach to Collieston I began to think that my troubles were behind me. I knew from the forecast that the wind was due to pick up through the day, but if it did I thought I would just land on some stretch of the seductive-looking beach.

No sooner had I started along the beach than the excitement of Girdle Ness together with too many cups of tea for breakfast resulted in an extended bladder. With the swell building and the wind picking up, I also wanted to stop sooner rather than later, not fancying a beach landing if conditions worsened further. Where the Don emptied into the sea up ahead there were already large breaking waves. Sediment carried down the river is deposited as it reaches the sea with the effect of making the confluence shallower than elsewhere. At the same time the river current carves an undulating pattern out of the sand on the seabed. When the force of the river flow meets the opposing force of the incoming waves over this uneven seabed the water is forced upwards, creating very big waves.

The line of waves stretched several hundred metres out to sea and I knew that I would have to take the long way round to avoid them, so I made up my mind to land before then. As I got closer to the beach I looked over my shoulders to see a huge wave gathering. It was not an odd breaking wave that could be easily avoided, it was a long unbroken surf wave whose unavoidable destiny was to crash onto the beach. It was about to sweep me up to share that destiny. I started back paddling furiously and managed to reverse over the first wave but the larger second wave picked me up. I began surfing it but was unable to keep a line with my stern rudder and ended up bracing on the wave as it crashed all around before passing under me. I turned quickly to face back out to sea, met the next wave face on and managed to power over the next and the next until I fought free of the break line. In the stramash I lost my deck pump and one pogie off the deck – small losses in relation to the potential seriousness of the situation I had found myself in. I still needed the toilet though.

Once past the River Don confluence I tried to find a gentler spot to land but I again found myself caught by the surf. This time a wave caught me as I was manoeuvring the kayak diagonally to the wave. In an attempt to back paddle over it my paddle got stuck on the opposite side of the kayak and the wave pushed the kayak over the stationary paddle, causing me to capsize. It was a schoolboy error – I should have surfed it. As I was upside down I knew that I had a few seconds of calm before the next wave picked me up for another hammering so I took advantage of it to set myself up to roll, which worked. I headed for the beach and made a successful landing.

As I gathered my thoughts I suddenly realised that I had landed at Balmedie, the very spot where the sea kayaker had drowned the month before. With my morale already fairly low I punished myself further with thoughts of how stupid and inconsiderate my presence there was. My performance in landing was like that of a tumbling clown. Thankfully the beach was fairly empty and I hoped that no-one had noticed my inept performance, more so that no-one was looking at me with futile hope.

Shivering on the beach, I had that very distinctive sensation of sea water running down my nose, something I had not experienced for a long time. When you capsize, water can be forced up your nasal passage and somehow defies gravity by staying there for a little while. At some point, though, gravity inevitably has its way and the water is released. There is no accounting for when this happens. Sometimes it happens straight away and sometimes some hours afterwards. I have been embarrassed on many occasions, standing in company long after surfing in the sea when the water releases without warning. Those in your company not familiar with what is happening tend to recoil in disgust as a torrent of snot and sea water is released and, if you are quick enough, streams into a waiting handkerchief.

I saw from the map that, with conditions as they were, I would not be able to land again until Collieston, as the dumping beach ran all the way. The forecast was for the wind to pick up to force six. The harbour at Collieston faces south and east so I was keen to get there as early in the day as possible. I decided I had enough time.

However, once launched the paddling got increasingly harder and scarier. It was nervy at first because the swell was coming from the north-east, which met the wind coming from the south-east. There was also the two-knot tide to paddle against. For the first hour or so this was manageable technically but I couldn't help imagining what would happen when the stronger winds came as forecast.

To start with I could see the swell coming from a long way offshore. My target (a spire at Collieston) would come in and out of view as the swell kept rolling through. When I was about half-way the wind picked up and the sea became very ragged. I was beginning to need the toilet again but knew it would have to wait. I was far enough from the shore that the waves were not breaking but being large and ragged I had to concentrate to make sure that my paddle movements were timely and that I was ready to brace when necessary.

As the wind picked up again to about a force four I began to wonder what it would be like landing at Collieston. I worked through my options. I realised that apart from landing on a dumping beach I had no other option so just had to focus on paddling well and dealing with Collieston when I got there. With about five kilometres to go the wind strengthened to a force five. For three hours I had paddled harder than at any time on the trip in an attempt to get to Collieston before the big winds. I was very tired. I wanted to close my eyes and make the whole thing go away but I knew when I opened them it would still be there. Then I realised that I did have my eyes closed. For a split second I had nodded off – I was more tired than I had thought.

I tried to open a bag of dried fruit from under the elastics on my deck and managed to get one piece before I had to put two hands back on the paddle for a brace as the plastic bag with my remaining food got swept away. The waves were very complicated. When I went diagonally across them I had to reach deep into a trough with my paddle to provide balance or forward momentum and also retract it ready for the approach of the next wave.

My hands became very cold – I had been alternating my one remaining pogie between my two hands, but now it was too rough to risk taking a hand off the paddle so they both had to stay as they were, the right one clad, the left one unclad. It was fortunate the way it worked out because my right hand is my controlling hand and therefore more important to keep warm. I realised that I was gripping the paddle much tighter than I should, which was helping to reduce the circulation to my fingers and making the cold and numbness worse. Good paddling requires a myriad of subtle movements to adjust to the challenges of each wave but these subtleties were not available to me. My hands had been gripping the paddle for so long they had become numb claws, locked vice-like around the paddle, leaving my fingers unresponsive and unable to make normal movement. In this sorry state I pulled abreast of the building with the spire high on the cliff at the approach to Collieston.

In calmer conditions it would have been possible to land on either side of the pier but as I drew near the southernmost side I saw that it was not a good option, so I continued for another two hundred metres to get a view of the landing on the northern side. This too seemed a poor option. I knew from my mapwork earlier that to continue up the coast would take me into further cliff areas with few landing opportunities. So with a force six blowing onshore, completely worn out, unable to paddle further and out of options I decided to land in the bay straight ahead of me and suffer the consequences.

It did not look promising as large waves sped shorewards and crashed against rocks either side of the approaches to the pier. I inched forwards, aware that a wave could easily pick me up and send me crashing onto the rocks. The waves got a little crazy as clapotis bounced off north and south shore rocks and met in the middle where I was. There were also skerries in the middle of the approach, so waves suddenly reared up and broke with astonishing power. I slalomed through these wild waves with as much care as I could muster and managed to keep a line of sorts. Eventually I felt the waves ease as I inched ever further into the mouth of the bay and then to a small sheltered spot to the right of the pier.

I know that a lot of people tend to cry when they are on solo trips and I wondered if it would happen to me. Instead I just kept thinking, 'I want to get off this "effing" water and get into warm dry clothes.' I had arrived having paddled for four hours against a two-knot tide and a weird, weird sea complicated by the southeast wind and big north-east swell. With signs of hypothermia already evident it was excruciatingly painful for me to get out of the kayak and walk around. With necessity being the mother of invention I put up my tent, changed into dry clothes and went for a walk to the local Post Office to buy a newspaper – I wanted to read about other people's problems as I'd had enough of my own. As I walked back from the Post Office I saw that the wind had picked up some more and, looking at the bay I had entered an hour ago, I knew that I would no longer have been able to land safely. I had bought a miniature of whisky at the Post Office and back in my tent I raised a toast to the puffins, my guardian angels, and gave thanks to Mara for allowing me back onto dry land (Mara is the Gaelic word for sea).

13

The end is nigh

I SPENT THE NIGHT CONFRONTED BY DEMONS. SLEEP DID NOT come easily with my mind as storm-tossed as the seas I had just survived. In the morning Jane arrived for the final re-supply of food and exchange of diary notes. I had not been looking forward to meeting her, concerned that she would see the fear in me and worry more.

I did what I could to be upbeat; we found a café with a power source to exchange the data. Jane had brought Farril and I sat in the boot of the estate car with him as Jane took a photograph (see photo 26, plate section). Many of the things I needed in life were right there in that car; there was no real need for me to continue the journey. It was never supposed to be about trials and tribulations. I had come to focus more on staying alive than contemplating sustainability. Since one of the main purposes of the journey was to write this book, I could easily have stopped at that point with plenty to write about.

With Jane about to leave I had to make the decision whether

to go or stay. I still can't fully explain why but even though I really did want to go home I still didn't want to give up. Some combination of fear of not finishing, pride and stubbornness had overtaken the original agenda. Yet those were not the characteristics I wanted to exhibit. Instead, I wanted to be seen as someone at peace with himself, trying humbly in some small way to make the world a better place.

My crisis of conscience became more marked when Jane returned me to my tent and I could see from the heavy seas that I would not be putting on the water today. We said our farewells and as they drove away I could see Jane looking in the rear view mirror and Farril looking at me from the back of the car. I don't remember any time in my life when I felt such strongly opposed emotions. A loud whistle would still have been enough to stop them...

Having just experienced company, being alone again was much more intense. The heavy rain and strong winds continued, so I decided to read in my tent. As daylight faded I opened a special package that Jane had left for me. In it was a half bottle of *Moët & Chandon* champagne from my parents-in-law for me to celebrate starting the last leg. Never one to let a bout of misery get in the way of a good party I tuned the radio to a folk music channel and popped the cork.

The next morning the sea state had not changed and the forecast suggested that the weather was to continue for at least another day. So it was a walk back to the Post Office to renew my acquaintance with Islay and Abbie. Islay had been the postmistress for forty-seven years. Post Offices, like butchers and bakers, are some of the last vestiges of once vibrant rural communities (in 2008 Collieston Post Office closed after over 100 years of service to the community). Their very existence is threatened by changing consumer patterns, as shoppers find it more convenient to buy at supermarkets. While the price of goods may well be lower at the supermarket checkout, this is an example of how growth economics affects rural communities. It is also an example of why GDP as a measure of society's standard of living takes no account of quality of life issues.

I was asked in for tea and biscuits. Afterwards, keen not to overstay my welcome, I walked around the lanes of Collieston to busy myself and keep my mind off the weather. I concentrated on looking at things that generally do not interest me. In this way someone's garden became fascinating. In between this prowling, and when I felt brave enough, I returned to the beach to look at the waves, trying to work out if I could launch. Sometimes I convinced myself that if I could only get through the narrow entrance between the rocks and harbour wall then I'd manage okay in the sea beyond. However, a walk along the cliff edge to look down at what I would encounter suggested otherwise. The day passed slowly.

The next day was no better but I was keen to take advantage of any change in the weather and so packed everything up. All morning I studied the waves, setting my stopwatch to work out how long it was between the waves I thought I could break through and the big ones that would back-flip me. Just when I thought I'd established a pattern, the timing changed. After a whole morning studying the waves the only pattern I could discern was that there was no fixed pattern, only a pattern of irregularity.

It did seem, though, that the wind had changed direction a little and that the harbour entrance might have been easier to get out of than where I was in Cransdale Bay. I emptied everything out of my kayak, took it over to the harbour and reloaded it ready to launch, only to find that I was imagining things. With waves breaking over the harbour wall I was not going to get out safely. With a sense of relief I carried everything back to my original camp spot and settled down for a third night. After three days of mounting despondency I detected something different about my thoughts. Now and then I had been thinking of myself in the past tense. How this came about worried me because I imagined the newspapers reporting the death of a second solo kayaker in the space of two months on the same stretch of coastline. 'How coincidental,' the newspaper headlines might pontificate. Yet I also thought of myself as a person that lives and breathes, thinks and feels. I didn't want to be a mere statistic that people talked about in the past tense. It was odd to have my whole being stripped away and be left with a reminder of mortality staring me in the face.

The next morning I was ready to launch at first light. I had been listening to the wind dropping through the night and I wanted to take advantage of the lull. The swell was still very big but now rounded, and launching from Cransdale Bay was quite straightforward. Till about a kilometre offshore the swell just picked me up then gently lowered me into the following trough. This was good because I started off paddling like a robot, stiff and nervous. I needed to relax and allow my kinaesthetic awareness to return. Without it I was like a cork sitting on the sea, at the whim of wind and current. The skerries called 'the Skares' were up ahead and I could see the swell crashing against them. From some way off it seemed that I would not need to go round them; there appeared to be a passage through the middle.

Soon I came abreast of the Bay of Cruden where the pipeline carrying North Sea oil comes ashore. Underneath me flowed fossil fuel that had lain trapped in sedimentary rock for millions of years. Within the next year or so it would become part of the atmosphere, adding yet more parts per million carbon to it. Soon afterwards Slains Castle, the inspiration for Bram Stoker's novel *Dracula*, passed behind my left shoulder. So too did the Bullers of Buchan, a dramatic cliff face of perpendicular rock. Not somewhere to get too close to with the swell. By the time I got to Boddam I had covered ten kilometres in one hour with tidal assistance. After a short break I returned to the water with growing apprehension as the forecast warned of increasing winds to force six. At least, coming from the south-west, it would be behind me, pushing me on.

All day there had been a lot of helicopter activity as people and equipment transferred from Aberdeen to the offshore oil rigs. Seeing and hearing them offered a sense of security, even though I knew that they probably would not see me if I got into difficulties. Just beyond Peterhead harbour a small creel boat called *Be Ready* closed in from behind. The skipper gave me a bit of a fright because with the noise of the wind I had not heard him approach. He asked if everything was all right, and I wondered if my nerves had become so frayed that they were instantly noticeable to anyone who saw me. I gave the skipper a thumbs up, guessing that local fishermen here were still remembering the lone sea kayaker lost at Balmedie.

With a following sea to help me on my way I surfed the waves formed by a very manageable force four wind. The lighthouse at Rattray Head gave me something to aim for. Two things were to happen when I got there. The first was that I would move from the inshore weather forecast area Rattray Head to Berwick-upon-Tweed, to the area Cape Wrath to Rattray Head, a sure sign of progress to the north. The second thing was that I would turn west into the Moray Firth. As soon as I did that the land itself would shelter me from the prevailing winds. So long as the wind stayed in the south I would be protected from the worst of its effects.

Because it was such a significant milestone I stopped to take some photographs. My favourite shows my kayak sitting on a sandy beach. In the far distance the lighthouse is framed by a light blue sky with delicate wispy clouds. It does not take a lot of imagination to think that it could be a Caribbean setting. Once again I marvelled at the beauty of my homeland and wondered if we really do need to spend so much time going on holiday to exotic places (see photo 27, plate section).

My journey was not just about encountering the land and seascape, it was about people too. I landed somewhere between St Combs and Inverallochy, looking to camp in the dunes. Two gentlemen out for their evening constitution stopped to pass the time of day (see photo 28, plate section). I estimated them to be in their seventies, but with their flat caps and walking sticks they looked the picture of health. They were curious about how such a fragile craft could manage in such difficult conditions. Not wanting to dwell on my own recent experiences I told them about Brian Wilson's book describing his epic journey around Scotland and how he paddled in force eight conditions. I could see they were impressed. To impress these guys was no mean achievement – they knew about life at sea, the hardship and the losses, the lifeboats and the rescues. The sea was in their blood. They told me about being brought up there – the decline of fishing and the growth of drug-taking among the young. It would be wrong to overstate the impressions gained from such a short meeting, but I did feel that in the middle of the chaos of a world looking for answers to the meaning of life there were two gentlemen who had found a large part of it. Perhaps in our culture we do not respect the wisdom of elders as much as we should.

Lying in my tent that night I calculated I had covered forty-eight kilometres that day. If the weather held I would be home very soon.

With an excellent forecast I was determined to get some miles under my belt. First I needed to pass the entrance to Fraserburgh harbour, the largest shellfish landing port in Europe and a busy thoroughfare. Just like the harbours at Aberdeen and Peterhead before, I got a little anxious with all the motorised craft coming and going, especially with me being so small and low in the water. I looked out the VHF radio to make sure it was switched on and ready to use. I also checked that my collision and mini-flares were handy before committing myself. The crossing went without incident and I breathed a sigh of relief once I moved out of the shipping lane vector.

Safely across, a sudden dose of lethargy set in. Perhaps I'd become a little ragged after the physical and mental stress of the last few days. I couldn't be bothered paddling, so I sat offshore a while and watched two young lads with golf drivers striking balls into the bay, staying out of range just in case of any accidents. I had to work hard to rouse myself out of the stupor. The sea was so calm and inviting. It was the sort of day I had been dreaming of while at my computer in the office waiting to get started. I provoked myself with a physical challenge to cover fifty kilometres in the day and, because the sea was so calm, to look out for whales and dolphins.

The landmarks began to appear and disappear as the day progressed. First Sandhaven, then Rosehearty, Quarry Head and into Pennan for a break. I had just kayaked along the most astonishing of coastlines with cliff faces one hundred metres high. The canoeist George Reid had told me to watch out for where the red sandstone cliffs abruptly stop and the grey metamorphic rock continues. The contrast was indeed striking. I could see the arches and caves that he had also told me about but, with a mission in hand, I acknowledged the wonderful landscape only cursorily.

With only a short stop at Pennan to see where *Local Hero* was filmed, I headed off once more, having left a donation for the harbour restoration fund. Further down the coast I could see the nesting birds that George mentioned. There too was Hell's Lum and Lion's Head, then on past Troup Head which, George explained, was the only mainland colony of gannets in Scotland. The sea off Troup Head was a little lumpy but still not too rough to prevent me from stopping to take photographs.

It was a magical place to be in such conditions. Gannets were taking off everywhere and heading out to sea to fish. Their brilliant white plumage caught the sun and flashed in the air as they plummeted seaward into shoals of fish. They swallow fish whole and have the ability to regurgitate them for their young. But there were great skuas (*Stercorarius skua*) around too, the pirates of the seabird world. Once they see gannets with a fish they pursue and harry them until the gannets either escape or are forced to regurgitate their catch, which the skuas then eat. It was not only fish on the skua's menu either. I have seen them attack and drown kittiwakes by holding them under the water. When the struggle is over the skua dismembers and eats the carcass. It is common to associate nature that is 'red in tooth and claw' with the African savannah, where lions hunt wildebeest and cheetahs chase down gazelles. But the predator-prey relationship that people pay a small fortune to experience on a tourist safari can be found in Scotland too.

Not for the first time on my journey I resolved to come back and spend more time in such a striking landscape. For the time being, though, I needed to be on my way. In haste I passed Gardenstown, More Head and Head of Garness to Macduff. The geography and geology along the coast is stunning, ranging from grassy cliffs, perpendicular rock faces, magnificent stone arches and amazing sculpted rock features to deeply recessed bays.

I was so intent on covering as much distance as possible that it was threatening to darken before I found a suitable campsite. In the distance I could see a caravan park at Boyndie Bay and opted for my first official campsite of the journey. It had been raining heavily for much of the day and it proved difficult finding a pitch not full of puddles. I ended up having to trust my groundsheet and set the tent up in the shallowest puddle I could find.

It had been another good day for distance: I had covered a little under my fifty kilometre target. I reflected on how much stronger I felt than when I started nearly a month ago. Whereas before my wrists had been weak, I could now push them through the cuffs of my dry cagoule with more ease. The paddle blades felt much smaller as I powered them through the water and the kayak seemed to glide gracefully and smoothly. Before, the paddle had felt heavy, the blades big and sluggish through the water and the kayak seemed to yaw from side to side.

Now I was fully focused on finishing the journey everything seemed secondary to the passing kilometres. The only thing that took higher priority was my own safety and although the wind was blowing force five, and gusting a little stronger, I was not so much frightened as careful. In any case the conditions were nowhere near as difficult as those at Collieston. I was protected from the southerly wind by sticking close to the land, but I still had to be careful not to take short cuts across the wider bays as I could easily be caught out far offshore. Focused on another fifty-kilometre day it was not long before I left behind Knock Head, East Head, and Portsoy, where marble was once quarried. It is still possible to visit the old quarry and pick up odd bits of marble. The French liked Portsoy marble for their fireplaces, one of the more famous being in the Palace of Versaille.

Sandend Bay, Logie Head and Cullen all disappeared over my left shoulder before I was stopped in my tracks by the sight of Bow Fiddle Rock at Portnockie, so called because it resembles a violin bow. It is quartzite rock that over time has been eroded and shaped by the ceaseless movement of waves. Despite my strong homing instinct I had to stop and dwell. In calmer conditions you could paddle through the arch, but the wind had moved round to the west and a strong swell was bouncing off the headland. As I edged round the headland I became increasingly exposed to the wind and I juddered to a halt when faced with its full ferocity. With no sign of it abating I continued paddling, strong and steady, inching towards Findochty. Just beyond the village I arrived, utterly exhausted, in a sheltered bay that provided an idyllic camp spot at the foot of some dunes.

With dry clothes on I went in search of a friend who lives in Findochty but he was not at home. Instead I found a pub in which to write up my diary and reflect on the day. It was distracting sitting in the pub with the boisterous noise of a crowded room, so I sought solace outside on a bench in the beer garden. Writing in the cold from the light of a head torch was much preferable.

The next morning I could hardly contain my excitement,

knowing how close Inverness was. I felt it important, though, to sit for a while and savour just being where I was. As I relaxed in a fold-away chair with a cup of hot tea I could hear song birds singing and I felt pretty comfortable with my own internal wellbeing. Creating the opportunity for this thought space had the desired effect. Although I was keen to move on with the journey, I reminded myself that a big physical and psychological transition was required when moving from the land to the sea. It meant leaving an environment that I felt comfortable and safe in for another environment that required different skills for me to be comfortable and safe in. As I had been finding out, adventurous experiences in themselves do not necessarily lead to a deeper awareness of the relational self. I comforted myself by thinking of the educational work I wanted to involve myself in as soon as the journey was over.

After much pondering I made the transition and headed for Buckie. Here the wave formation reminded me of the half pipe that skateboarders and snowboarders use; I found myself careering up one side then the other. Once past the mouth of the River Spey I stopped at a storm beach that ran all the way to Lossiemouth, a distance of around ten kilometres. It reached around fifteen feet tall from the low water mark to its highest point, and shelved very steeply. Luckily there was no onshore wind when I reached it. Had the wind been blowing strongly from the north it would not have been easy to land there or anywhere along its boulder-strewn length: a ten kilometre 'no landing area' within the confines and safety of the Moray Firth! (See photo 29, plate section.)

At Lossiemouth I was reminded by the harbour master that I shouldn't be using the harbour for access and egress, but he was kind enough to leave me be since I had hauled the kayak onto a pontoon. After a short coffee stop I pushed on knowing that I was within two days of Inverness. At Hopeman I stopped for a while to watch an instructor teaching novices how to surf their kayaks. I was struck with a bout of nostalgia, remembering my own fun days as a novice thrashing around in the surf. The nostalgia was interrupted as I passed under the flight path of RAF jets taking off. I had to clasp my hands to my ears to shut out the worst of the noise. But keeping noise out of my ears was not the only bodily intrusion – shockwaves thundered through the air, sending vibrations passing through sinew, muscle and bone, shaking me to the core.

A high-pressure system had moved in, with the promise of a windless evening and an opportunity to watch the sun sink below the horizon. I knew now that barring incident, accident or bad weather I would be in Inverness the day after to end the journey. As it would be my last night I chose the beautiful setting of Culbin Woods at the mouth of Findhorn Bay to camp.

The setting was exquisite. The River Findhorn meets the sea at what must be one of most beautiful estuaries anywhere. Seals were on the hunt for salmon and sea trout. A narrow channel links the sea with Findhorn Bay a little upstream. Water is funnelled through the channel created by lines of sand, one of which continues along the east coast where I had just come from, and the other leads west to where I was heading. In the distance the picturesque village of Findhorn appeared tranquil and inviting. I resisted the temptation to paddle over for a celebratory drink because I wanted to savour the moment by myself.

I thought of my guardian angels, the puffins, and how they had watched over me (see photo 30, plate section). The wind was present, but not quite the ferocity experienced at Collieston, and I welcomed its gentler side. The sea was moving and restless as always. The sea and the wind reminded me of lovers whose moods range from stormy passion to gentle intimacy. I had been caught up in their passions for a month and I had felt the intensity of that relationship. I felt like a third wheel, tolerated but not needed. The relationship between wind and wave invokes in me a sense of respect, wonder, curiosity, awe, and at times fear.

Because the wind and sea were on their best behaviour I was able to hear more clearly the call of a duck. I had seen it often through the day but had never been close enough to get a good look. I could hear its very distinctive call, which sounded something like 'ow, ow, owal-ow.' I later identified it as a longtailed duck.

More of my trip companions made an appearance. Seals, gulls and the midges… who tested to the limit any ecocentric principles suggesting that they too had rights. I was reminded of childhood experiences among Caledonian Pines, of one of my earliest memories climbing their flaky lower branches. The fragrance of resin is far sweeter than any perfume I have ever smelled.

I was happy to bathe in nostalgia. I knew that with the physical journey coming to an end I would soon return to the life I had temporarily left behind. I resolved that when I did I would not judge myself on the thoughts and feelings that occupied me throughout the journey, but rather I would concentrate on using them as a motivating factor in my own life and in influencing others about the importance of action.

With my tent up and clothes hanging out to dry on tree branches I did something that I had been wanting to do since Collieston – I phoned Jane and asked her to meet me tomorrow to take me home.

In the morning after an evening of high pressure there will often be haar around. It seemed a fitting climax that this turned out to be the case on both my last and first day. The haar was a pea-souper and I could not see more than twenty metres in front of me. Not only did the haar deprive me of vision but it affected sound too. Consequently it was difficult to hear where the waves were landing on the beach. Deprived of both of sight and sound I thought of myself getting lost, going round and round in circles in the supposedly straightforward terrain of the Moray Firth. For the first time on the journey I had to take a bearing on my compass to determine a direction of travel.

The haar burned off as I approached Nairn. I travelled onwards around Whiteness Head, then between the narrows at Fort George and Chanonry Point. It was early afternoon when I pulled ashore at Ardersier where Jane joined me for the last ten kilometres. We had planned some time ago to paddle the last stretch together. I thought it fitting because Jane loves to sea paddle and I wanted her to be part of at least some of the journey (see photo 31, plate section).

As we crossed the Inner Basin of the Moray Firth the wind picked up and peaked at around force four. We were both relieved that the wind peaked there, not wanting to have an epic on the last day. Eventually the tide carried us round the corner to North Kesock where Jane's parents waited to greet us.

Looking back at photographs of that moment it is pleasing to see myself smiling happily in them despite the fear of the week before. The mouth of the River Ness is in the background, where the journey began on a cold April Fools' Day. A deeply bronzed face looks back from the photograph, reminding me of the external effects of the journey as the sun imprinted its presence upon me. What are not visible though are the changes that happened inside (see photo 32, plate section).

Epilogue

MY HOUSE OVERLOOKS THE CAIRNGORM MOUNTAINS. I often sit looking out of the window daydreaming, thinking and looking for answers to the questions that always seem to appear. On this occasion I looked up from writing on my laptop to see the plateau covered with a light dusting of mid-summer snow. It is unusual to have so much snow in June so far down the mountain; thinking through why this might be provided a welcome distraction from concentrating on writing. However, the pause between writing is also a pause between thoughts – the opportunity to shift focus from one reality to another. In that moment it dawned on me that this short episode was a microcosm of what I experienced on my journey – a concentrated period that provided an opportunity to shift focus from everyday life to look at things from different perspectives.

The idea to *Canoe around the Cairngorms* came during one long winter night as I pored over maps looking for something that might catch the public's attention more for its purpose than its achievement. As the route began to reveal itself on the map so too did some transcendental themes such as the mystery of mountains, the allure of the sea and journeying into the unknown. If these alone were not enough to raise interest the idea of canoeing around a landlocked mountain range might raise the odd eyebrow. Then, I thought, those aware of Thoreau's writing might be interested that this was to be a circumnavigation of my home. I had set out to discover what he meant when he challenged us all to look for inspiration in landscapes close to our homes and then to live deliberately in them. But for what purpose?

I have tried to present an alternative discourse to the 'doom and gloom' accounts of the exploitative and harmful effects of humans on the environment. We are now more than ever aware of global climate change and loss of biodiversity. However, the problem with so much bad news is that most people often don't know how to relate to these things when they are presented negatively and in a 'finger pointing' sort of way. When we talk about sustainability we tend to focus on the destructive effects of humanity and less about our creativity and problem-solving abilities. I just wondered if some of the solutions to the problems could be found by focusing more on the joyous aspects of human potential. But, if humans are to be agents of change, by what means could this potential be tapped?

It has become clear to me that knowledge of these things, although an excellent start point, is not enough. There is a need to consider different sorts of motivating factors that might translate these thoughts into actions. This led me to consider the question: 'If people spent more time outdoors would the beauty and inspiration of the land and seascape provide sufficient motivation to lead more sustainable lifestyles?'

I know that journeys like mine can be little more than self-indulgent adventures. I believe, though, that experiences such as these and outdoor experiences in general do have transformative potential. I was deeply touched by my own journey. The integration of thought and deep experience of outdoor places has been direct and compelling and fuelled my passion to understand and improve this precarious relationship that we human beings have with the rest of our planet. The crux, though, is understanding that all things are related, and then believing that somewhere within this web of relationships there is room for each of us to make a difference. Of course our spheres of influence will change from time to time or place to place, and some of us will have greater spheres of influence than others. But the point is pretty straightforward – we are all in this together and so if not you, then who? If not I, then why?

When all is said and done my quest can be summarised quite succinctly. Sensorial immersion can provide deep experiential engagement with the world around us. Evolution has provided our species with an incredible capacity for emotional and intellectual introspection and creativity. The outdoors provides spaces and places in which to nurture this combination of deep experience and deep thought. However, the potential will not be realised until it is translated into action. In other words the journey is never over.

References

Some material in this book has featured in part in the following publications:

Nicol, R. (2003). *Outdoor education: research topic or universal value?* Part three. Journal of Adventure Education and Outdoor Learning, 3 (1), 11-27.

Nicol, R. (2014). *Entering the Fray: The Role of Outdoor Education in Providing Nature-Based Experiences that Matter.* Educational Philosophy and Theory, 46 (5), 449-461.

Nicol, R. (2015). *In the name of the whale.* In: *Seascapes: Shaped by the sea*, Eds M. Brown and B. Humberstone. Ashgate. 141-153.

Chapter One

Page 21 – Brody, H. (2002). *The other side of eden: hunter-gatherers, farmers and the shaping of the world.* London: Faber and Faber, 254.

Page 22 – Capra, F. (1983). *The turning point: science, society and the rising culture.* London: Flamingo, 47.

Page 24 – Mason, B. (1984). *Path of the paddle.* Leicester: Cordee, 3.

Chapter Two

Page 33 – McNeil, J. (2000). *Something new under the sun: an environmental history of the twentieth century.* London: Penguin, 19.

Page 34 – Suzuki, D. (1993). *Time to change.* NSW, Australia: Allen and Unwin, 120.

Page 39 – Naess, A. (2002). *Life's philosophy, reason and feeling in a deeper world.* Athens: University of Georgia Press, 2-3.

Chapter Three

Page 48 – Stern, N. (2006). *The economics of climate change. Executive Summary.* (available online), i.

Page 53 – Mason, B. (1984). *Path of the paddle.* Leicester: Cordee, 3.

Page 53 – Schumacher, E.F. (1974). *Small is beautiful.* London: Abacus, 10-11.

Page 56 / 58 – Porritt, J. (2005). *Capitalism as if the world matters.* London: Earthscan, 3.

Chapter Four

Page 66 – Farndon, J. (1998). *Concise encyclopedia Earth.* London: Dorling Kindersley, 80.

Page 73 – Mackean, D. and Jones, B. (1975). *Introduction to human and social biology.* London: John Murray, 40.

Page 75 – Lovelock, J. (2007). *The revenge of Gaia.* London: Penguin, 173.

Chapter Five

Page 80 – Olsen, S. (1958). *Listening Point.* Minneapolis: University of Minnesota, 74.

Page 85 – Max-Neef, M. (1986). *Human-scale economics: the challenges ahead.* In P. Ekins (Ed). *The living economy: a new economics in the making* (45-54). London: Routledge and Kegan Paul, 52.

Page 85 – Robertson, J. (1986). *The mismatch between health and economics.* In P. Ekins (Ed). *The living economy: a new economics in the making* (113-121). London: Routledge and Kegan Paul, 114.

Chapter Six

Page 104 – Capra, F. (1996). *The web of life.* London: HarperCollins, 5-6.

Chapter Seven

Page 114 – Monbiot, G. (2007). *Heat.* London: Penguin, 3.

Page 114 – Gore, A. (2006). *An inconvenient truth.* London: Bloomsbury, 26.

Page 115 – *IPCC Fourth Assessment Report. Climate Change 2007: Synthesis Report. Summary for Policymakers.* Cambridge: Cambridge University Press.

Page 117 – Stern, N. (2006). *The economics of climate change. Executive Summary.* (available online), iii.

Page 118 – Lynas, M. (2007). *Six degrees.* London: HarperCollins, 30.

Page 118 – IPCC Fourth Assessment Report. *Climate Change 2007: Synthesis Report. Summary for Policymakers.* Cambridge: Cambridge University Press, 12.

Page 119 – Monbiot, G. (2007). *Heat.* London: Penguin, xxi.

Page 120 – Lynas, M. (2007). *Six degrees.* London: HarperCollins, 207.

Page 121 – Monbiot, G. (2007). *Heat.* London: Penguin, 22.

Page 122 – *ibid.* xxi-xxii.

Chapter Eight

Page 134 – Smyth, J. (1995). *Environment and education: A view of a changing scene,* 1 (1), 3-19, 18.

Page 134 – Orr, D. (1992). *Ecological literacy: education and the transition to a postmodern world.* Albany: State University of New York Press.

Page 134 – Brennan, A. (1994). *Environmental literacy and educational ideal.* Environmental Values, 3 (1), 3-16, 3.

Page 137 – Orr, D. (1992). *Ecological literacy: education and the transition to a postmodern world.* Albany: State University of New York Press, 5.

Page 139 – Geddes, P. (1902). *Nature study and geographical education.* In *Scottish Geographical Journal* (525-536) 18 (10), 530.

Page 140 – Searby, P. (1989). *The new school and the life of Cecil Reddie (1858-1932) and the early years of Abbotshome school.* History of Education 18(1), 1-21, 17.

Chapter Nine

Page 153 – Suzuki, D. (1997). *The sacred balance.* NSW, Australia: Allen and Unwin, 102.

Page 154 – Weston, A. (1994). *Back to Earth: tomorrow's environmentalism.* Philadelphia: Temple, 82.

Page 155 – Bloom, B. S., Krathwohl, D. R. and Masia, B. B. (eds) (1964). *Taxonomy of Educational Objectives: Book 2 Affective Domain.* London: Longman, 45.

Page 156 – Gardner, H. (1993). *Frames of mind: the theory of multiple intelligences (2nd edition).* London: Fontana.

Page 156 / 7 – Gardner, H. (1999). *Intelligence reframed: multiple intelligences for the 21st century.* New York: Perseus Books Group, 41-43.

Page 160 – Fromm, E. (1993). *The art of being.* London: Constable, 25.

Page 162 – Goleman, D. (2004). *Emotional intelligence & working with emotional intelligence (omnibus).* London: Bloomsbury, 40.

Chapter Ten

Page 166 – Ryle, G. (1990). *The concept of mind.* London: Penguin, 110.

Page 178 – Naess, A. (1989). *Ecology, community and lifestyle.* Cambridge: Cambridge University Press.

Page 178 – Suzuki, D. (1997). *The sacred balance.* NSW, Australia: Allen and Unwin, 130.

Page 179 – Horwood, B. (1991). *Tasting the berries: Deep ecology and experiential education.* Journal of Experiential Education (23-26), 14 (3), 23.

Page 179 – Horwood, B. (1995). *Tasting the berries: deep ecology and experiential education.* In Kraft, R. and Keilsmeiner, J. (eds). *Experiential Schools and Higher Education* (106-112). Iowa: Kendall Hunt.

Page 180 – Capra, F. (2002). *The hidden connections.* London: HarperCollins, 200-201.

Chapter Eleven

Page 203 – Wilson, B. (1988). *Blazing paddles: a Scottish coastal odyssey.* Oxford: Oxford Illustrated Press.